Coalmining Women

Victorian lives and campaigns

Angela V. John

Cambridge University Press

Cambridge

New York   New Rochelle

Melbourne   Sydney

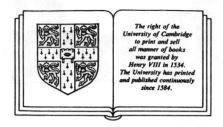

The right of the
University of Cambridge
to print and sell
all manner of books
was granted by
Henry VIII in 1534.
The University has printed
and published continuously
since 1584.

Published by the Press Syndicate of the University of Cambridge
The Pitt Building, Trumpington Street, Cambridge CB2 1RP
32 East 57th Street, New York, NY 10022, USA
10 Stamford Road, Oakleigh, Melbourne 3166, Australia

First published 1984
Fourth printing 1989

Printed in Great Britain by the University Press, Cambridge

Library of Congress catalogue card number: 84–7663

British Library cataloguing in publication data

John, Angela
Coalmining women. – (Women in history)
1. Women coal-miners – Great Britain – History — 19th century
I. Title   II. Series
331.4′822334′0941   HD6073.M62G7
ISBN 0 521 27872 4

Acknowledgements

The author and publisher would like to thank the following for permission to reproduce illustrations:
front cover, pp. 23, 29 (below) Wigan Record Office; title page, pp. 10, 15, 19, 22, 25, 26 (left and right), 29, 37 The Master and Fellows of Trinity College, Cambridge; p. 7 (above) John Hannavy, Wigan College of Technology; pp. 9, 16, 34, 36 Mary Evans Picture Library; pp. 13, 17 (below) the Controller of H.M. Stationery Office (Crown Copyright documents from the Public Record Office); pp. 18 (above), 24 (above) Mrs M. Wemyss; pp. 18 (below), 20 British Library Newspaper Library, Colindale; p. 24 (below) Peter Clarkson; p. 39 Polly Gee; p. 40 (left) Anglo-Chinese Educational Institute; p. 40 (right) Barbara Angle.

Thanks are due to the John Rylands University Library of Manchester and to the Central Services Unit of Thames Polytechnic for supplying prints of illustrations from the 1842 Children's Employment Commission and the *Prescot Reporter.*

Cover illustration: Women at the pit head, Strangeways Hall, Platt Bridge
Title page: Munby and a Wigan pit girl

Cover design by Pavel Büchler

Further details of illustrations and source materials:

title page	Munby collection 113[1e(ii)]
p. 4	Parliamentary Paper 1842 xviii p. 61
p. 5	P.P. 1845 xlii p. 197
p. 6	P.P. 1842 xvi p. 383
p. 7 (below)	P.P. 1842 xvi p. 387
p. 10	Munby 110[11(2)]
p. 13	PRO ref. H.O. 45/511 X56673
p. 15	Munby 118[22]
p. 17 (below)	PRO ref. RG 9/2769
p. 18 (below)	*The Graphic* no. 463 12/10/1878
p. 19	Munby 120[16]
p. 20	*The Pictorial World,* 11 April 1874
p. 21	P.P. 1867, Command No 3768 p. 578
p. 22	Munby 110[17] fol. 11r
p. 23	Wickham collection
p. 25	Munby 97[1] fol. 86v
p. 26 (left)	Munby 111[8e], (right) 121[35]
p. 28	J. B. Mannix, *Mines and their story* 1913
p. 29	Munby 113[8b]
p. 31	*Prescot Reporter,* 11 December 1886
p. 37	Munby 57[e] (loose leaf in diary)
p. 44	Original text from broadside by Harkness of Preston (Maddon Collection) in *Poverty Knock,* ed. Roy Palmer, Cambridge University Press 1974.

Contents

A note on money in this book

£1 = 20s (shillings)
1s = 12d (pence)
The old shilling has become 5 new pence. Remember that the value of money was very different in the nineteenth century. To work out the real value you should compare the wages people received with how much they had to pay for food, rent, etc.

I would like to thank all those who have helped in the publication of this book, especially Penny Rudge, Lisa Owen Jones, the late Alf Clarkson, Cyril Park, Eric Humphreys and Hazel Humphreys. Special thanks to the editors Carol Adams, Paula Bartley and Cathy Loxton and to Graham Hart and Ruth Foster at Cambridge University Press.

1 In search of women miners

Background

Today all Britain's coalminers are men. The only women to be seen at a colliery are the canteen staff, office cleaners and secretaries. Since the Sex Discrimination Act of 1975 (see Key dates page 41) women doctors have been permitted to give emergency treatment below ground but no woman can be employed as a miner underground. The ban does not include work done above ground but no women now work with coal on the *surface* (see glossary of terms page 41) either. This has not always been so.

At the beginning of the nineteenth century when the rapidly-expanding coal industry was the key to Britain's industrial development, her workforce consisted of men, women, boys, and girls and it is thought that at least 5,000 out of the total workforce of about 150,000 were females. This book looks at how and why the situation changed so that today no coalmining women remain.

The second chapter will look at the conditions of work for those labouring underground until the Mines and Collieries Act of 1842 forbade such work. We shall then explore the fortunes of those employed on the surface, (above ground) in the second half of the nineteenth century. The lesser known work of these pit brow lasses, as they were called, involved sorting and transporting coal in conditions very different from those in which underground workers had toiled. Many people, though, failed to realize the difference in the women's work. In order to find out what female surface work was like and how well it suited women, we shall see it through the eyes of a real Victorian pit lass, Jane Brown. We shall then follow the story of the women's fight to keep their jobs in the 1880s, looking at the issue from the viewpoint of the woman who organised the pit lasses, Margaret Park, the Mayoress of Wigan.

Although both women lived in Wigan, we shall see that the life of the middle-class lady was very different from that of Jane, the pit brow lass. Learning about the campaign in support of the pit women reveals much more than the lives of pit women and the efforts of 'do gooders' to organise a *pressure group*; it also informs us about the differences in the lifestyles of middle- and working-class women and raises wider questions about women's work more generally. It tells us about conditions for all mine workers, both male and female, in a major nineteenth-century industry. In addition we can discover the views of interested groups such as the coalowners and the early *women's movement*. We can explore the attitudes of trades unionists and see what the press thought.

The Lancashire pit brow lasses' struggle to continue working was a success story. Yet the issues it raises about women's work are still curiously relevant today.

Evidence

The material used in this book is based on a wide range of documents and other sources dating from the nineteenth century. It is useful to know what these sources are and how helpful they can be in finding out about the past. Here are a dozen different kinds of sources which have been used in putting together *Coalmining Women*.

1 The Census

Ever since 1801 a ten-yearly count has been made of the population of England and Wales. This is very useful, because, from it we can discover both the size and pattern of the population at different times and in different areas (see example page 17) and we can get information about mining jobs from 1841 onwards. We can also look at the details of individual families and households and so learn something about Jane Brown and other pit women.

2 Hansard

Another very helpful source is Hansard, the detailed record of what MPs say in Parliament.

From this we can read about major debates concerning the pit women (see page 9).

3 Official reports
In the nineteenth century many investigations were made into the type of work that people did. The Children's Employment Commission was one of the first major enquiries and it covered a range of industries in which children were employed. It was set up in 1840 by Parliament which established an enquiry called a *Royal Commission* to look, first of all, at mining. The Sub-Commissioners who reported on different parts of the country were so shocked by the conditions of adult females as well as those of the children that they included reports on women as well as on boys and girls (see page 9). As a result of the publicity which the report produced, Lord Ashley, later to become the Earl of Shaftesbury, introduced a Mines and Collieries bill which was passed in August 1842. This forbade the employment underground of all females and of boys under ten. We can learn how it was put into operation from the yearly reports of the Commissioner of Mines, H. S. Tremenheere. For later years there are also the area reports of the Inspectors of Mines which give information about pit brow lasses and sadly reveal stories of accidents (see pages 20 to 21). Parliament set up a small body called a Select Committee in 1865–7 to investigate mining and, in particular, questions of safety.

4 Home Office papers
Some women continued to work illegally after the law had been passed and we can gain some information about this from the letters sent to the Home Secretary (the person in charge of the department of government concerned with internal British affairs, called the Home Office). Tremenheere had to report to the Home Secretary.

5 Family papers
Tremenheere's own family papers help us to discover more information. Useful too are the family papers and general correspondence of coalowners as they reveal the viewpoints of the employers. For example Lord Francis Egerton's papers tell us a lot about affairs within the Worsley collieries in Lancashire (see page 12).

6 Diaries
Diaries can be a very valuable source for historians and give a special insight into the particular views of the person writing. Ashley kept a diary which helps us in trying to understand his motives and feelings about women's colliery work. This is useful to set alongside his public speeches. His full name was Anthony Ashley Cooper and he lived from 1801 to 1885. He was the Tory MP for the County of Dorset. He continually involved himself in the fortunes of the poor and needy even though he was from a privileged background himself. He had already led the struggle for factory reform and in 1842 campaigned to remove females from underground colliery work. He became the 7th Earl of Shaftesbury in 1851.

Perhaps, however, the diaries which are most interesting are those which reveal details of everyday life which have previously been neglected. From the diaries and notebooks of Arthur Joseph Munby (1828–1910) we can learn about Munby's preoccupation with the lives of working women. Munby was a Victorian gentleman from a respected family of Yorkshire lawyers. He too was a lawyer, a *barrister* by training, but although he lived alongside other barristers in the Inner Temple in London, he earned his living as a clerk for the *Ecclesiastical Commission*. Many of his friends were well-known figures in the literary, artistic and social circles of London. Yet, unknown to almost all his friends, Munby was secretly married to his servant, Hannah. He knew this Shropshire woman for 19 years before he married her and she had been in service in many different households before moving to Munby's.

Munby's chief 'hobby' in life was meeting and recording details of the lives of working-class women. He devoted all his spare time, energy and money to investigating the lives of women like Hannah. He was especially fascinated by work which was thought unsuitable for women, Such work contrasted strongly with the lifestyles of the genteel, fashionable ladies he encountered in 'polite society'. He travelled round Britain and Europe, filling his diaries with minute and unique observations of women brick workers, fisher girls, prostitutes, agricultural workers – indeed any women doing unusual or strenuous jobs. His favourites were, however, the pit brow lasses and it is thanks to Munby that it is possible to piece together the lives of women like Jane Brown.

7 Poetry, novels, folk song

Munby was known to his fashionable London friends as a minor poet. We can learn a little about pit girls from his and other peoples' poetry (see page 10) and also gain something from the folk songs of the time (see the story of Polly Parker on page 8). Novels and stories about pit women are another way of understanding their lives, or at least what writers thought about them. Frances Hodgson Burnett, best known for her children's stories such as *The Secret Garden* made the pit women the subject of her first full-length novel called *That Lass O'Lowrie's*.

8 Visual Material: maps, sketches, paintings and photographs

Maps can help to locate the coalfields, the places where colliery women worked and where the nearest towns were; sketches can also help. Munby sketched pit girls and arranged for many of them to have their photographs taken. A large number of pictures of pit lasses have survived and they can provide a number of useful clues about their lives. Some show details of work and clothes, some also suggest that the pit women became objects of curiosity (see page 26). The publicity which they received in the 1880s increased this tendency. They were also the subject of a painting exhibited at the Royal Academy in London at the time of their visit to the Home Office.

It is also important to remember that, for one reason or another, much gets destroyed over time. We can never recapture History completely. A thorough search has been made for a picture of Margaret Park, yet even her descendants have been unable to unearth one. Newspapers do, however, show her husband during his time of office as Mayor.

9 Newspapers and magazines

Many of the pictures of pit women appeared in newspapers and journals in the 1880s. Newspapers are a very rich source for the historian though it is important to find out the political views of a paper and try to see how papers with different viewpoints or emphasis handled the same story. Local papers are illuminating, as well as national newspapers such as *The Times*. Papers can fill in the background of other contemporary events as well as telling us about the pit women. Specialist journals can provide useful extra slants. Such papers include *The Colliery Guardian* and the *Women's Suffrage Journal*.

10 Trades Union and other specialist collections

The records of organisations such as the Trades Union Congress (founded in 1868) are helpful in presenting a different view to that of coalowners given in their records and papers.

11 Books and Pamphlets written at the time

Accounts written at the time enable us to understand the changes that were taking place in coalmining and other industries. We can begin to get a broader social and economic picture by reading as widely as possible. Autobiographies, like diaries, give highly personal accounts, but can help us get closer to how people felt. The biographies of people such as Ashley are informative too. Recent interest in women's history also means that we can now discover through history books rather more about the lives of women who have for so long been the silent half of the past's population.

12 Oral history

One of the most fascinating ways of bringing History alive is to interview elderly people. It helps to fill in some of the missing gaps in our knowledge and adds personal touches which can be highly significant. Some former pit women are still living, though most are very old. Their reminiscences have provided a unique and vital human voice in discovering the experiences of coalmining women.

2 Down the pit

Margaret Park investigates the past

It is a cold, windy evening in March 1886. Margaret Park, the Mayoress of Wigan, is slightly sorry that she has to go out. It would be far more cosy to sit in front of the blazing fire. Yet the thought of that fire sharply reminds her that she must leave the house. Long before the coal ever reached her gracious drawing room it would have been handled and sorted by women whose jobs are now in danger. She is about to chair a large meeting called in order to defend the rights of these pit brow lasses to work. She will make a short speech and urge people to sign a petition protesting against the proposed ban on women's employment at the surface of collieries.

Before going out Margaret decides to have one final look at the notes she has been making about the history of women's mining work. She has recognised for some time that the pit lasses she knows have a much easier life than their mothers who worked underground. It is only recently, though, that she has unravelled the story of those earlier coalmining women who had been banned from underground employment in mines in 1842. This is what she discovered.

Early history

Coalmining in Britain has a long history. The early mines of the thirteenth century were little more than holes tunnelled into hills or river banks but by the fifteenth century as well as these *drift mines*, *shafts* were being sunk to get out more coal. Families worked together in mines – fathers, mothers, daughters and sons. They tended to have their own tasks, with the females generally helping to transport the coal. A shortage of timber in Elizabethan times boosted the demand for coal and it was soon used in new industries such as glassmaking. Deeper shafts, however, meant greater risk of *damp* and explosion, and, although the smelting

Ann Ambler and Will Dyson being wound up the pit by an old woman. A drawing from the Children's Employment Commission Report of 1842.

of iron with coal helped to revolutionise the industry in the eighteenth century, the dangers and primitive methods of working remained. One way of raising miners for example was by using a *windlass*. A rope would be wound round a wooden drum and turned by hand as you can see in the picture where an old woman is pulling two children up the shaft.

Victorian Britain was very dependent on 'King Coal'. Eighty per cent of the world's coal was supplied by Britain. The industry provided coal fires for a much increased population. The introduction of steam machinery, the development of the railways and inventions such as gas street-lighting all pointed towards coalmining being one of the biggest growth industries of the nineteenth century.

Opposite: Britain in 1842

Scots coalfields produced one-third of the national output. The North-East had some very large concerns employing several thousand people. In most areas the size was nearer to an average of 30. Many had less than 12 although bigger coal mines were becoming more common.

OUTLINE MAP
OF THE
MINING DISTRICTS
of the
United Kingdom:
in which investigations have been made under the
CHILDREN'S EMPLOYMENT COMMISSION.
1842.

MINING DISTRICTS & NAMES OF THE SUB-COMMISSIONERS BY WHOM THEY WERE
RESPECTIVELY VISITED FOR THE PURPOSES OF THE CHILDRENS EMPLOYMENT INQUIRY

COAL AND IRON MINES.

	COAL FIELDS.	SUB-COMMISSIONERS.
I	SOUTH STAFFORDSHIRE (INCLUDING IRON MINES)	James Mitchell, Esq. LL.D
II	NORTH STAFFORDSHIRE (CHEADLE & THE POTTERIES)	Samuel S. Scriven, Esq
III	SHROPSHIRE (COALBROOKDALE, INCLUDING IRON MINES)	James Mitchell, Esq. LL.D
IV	WARWICKSHIRE	James Mitchell, Esq. LL.D
V	LEICESTERSHIRE	James Mitchell, Esq. LL.D
VI	DERBYSHIRE (INCLUDING IRON MINES)	John Michael Fellows, Esq
VII	WEST RIDING OF YORKSHIRE (SOUTHERN PART)	Jelinger C. Symons, Esq.
VIII	BRADFORD AND LEEDS (INCLUDING IRON MINES)	William Rayner Wood, Esq
IX	HALIFAX	S. Scriven, Esq.
X	LANCASHIRE and CHESHIRE	John L. Kennedy, Esq
XI	OLDHAM	Joseph Fletcher, Esq.
XII	NORTH OF LANCASHIRE	Antony Austin, Esq.
XIII	CUMBERLAND	Jelinger C. Symons, Esq. and Thomas Martin, Esq.
XIV	SOUTH DURHAM	James Mitchell, Esq. LL.D
XV	NORTH DURHAM AND NORTHUMBERLAND	John Roby Leifchild, Esq.
XVI	EAST of SCOTLAND (INCLUDING IRON MINES)	Robert Hugh Franks, Esq.
XVII	WEST of SCOTLAND (INCLUDING IRON MINES)	Thomas Tancred, Esq
XVIII	NORTH WALES (INCLUDING IRON MINES)	R. Herbert Jones, Esq.
XIX	SOUTH WALES & MONMOUTHSHIRE (INCLUDING IRON MINES)	Robert Hugh Franks, Esq. and Rhys William Jones, Esq.
XX	FOREST of DEAN (INCLUDING IRON MINES)	Elijah Waring, Esq.
XXI	SOUTH GLOUCESTERSHIRE	Elijah Waring, Esq.
XXII	NORTH SOMERSETSHIRE	Leonard Stewart, Esq. M.D.
XXIII	IRELAND	Frederick Roper, Esq. and Thomas Martin, Esq.

TIN, COPPER, LEAD & ZINC MINES.

	DISTRICTS IN WHICH VEINS ARE WROUGHT	SUB-COMMISSIONERS.
XXIV	CORNISH DISTRICT	Charles Barham, Esq. M.D.
XXV	ALSTON MOOR DISTRICT	James Mitchell, Esq. LL.D.
XXVI	FLINTSHIRE DISTRICT (NORTH WALES)	R. Herbert Jones, Esq.
XXVII	DERBYSHIRE	John Michael Fellows, Esq.
XXVIII	LEADHILLS (SCOTLAND)	Joseph Fletcher, Esq.
XXIX	IRELAND (VARIOUS DISTRICTS)	Frederick Roper, Esq. and Thomas Martin, Esq.

NOTE

The Roman Numerals refer to the names of the several Districts
and of the Sub Commissioners who have visited them, inscribed in the margin.
The darker Tint ▓▓ marks the Coal and Iron Mining Districts.
The lighter Tint ▒▒ marks the Tin, Copper, Lead & Zinc Mining Districts.

The coalfields and women's work in 1842

By 1842 there were already 2,000 collieries scattered over Britain. The coalfields stretched from Scotland to Somerset but were mainly in the central part of the country. It is difficult to know exactly how many people worked in coalmining as the 1841 Census is incomplete. By the 1840s there were about four times as many workers as there had been at the start of the century; by 1841 there may well have been as many as 150,000 workers: five or six thousand of whom would have been female. Although the females were a small proportion of the total workforce they were concentrated in certain coalfields and so formed a significant part of the mine workers in those areas.

As the table shows, the four major female-employing districts were east Scotland, Yorkshire, west Lancashire and south Wales. A few other areas had small numbers – there were some female horse drivers in Cumberland for example. Women no longer worked in the north-eastern pits and where the industrial revolution was creating new jobs for women (for example in the woollen trade in Yorkshire) women were leaving mining. It remained, on the whole, a family affair.

The male collier *hewed* or extracted the coal below ground, assisted by the *drawers* or putters. In some of the smaller pits women and girls pulled baskets or tubs of coal along low passages, harnessed by *belt and chain*, as in the picture. In the more modern pits, wheeled tubs were pushed along pit floors fitted with cast iron rails. In those where ponies pulled the loads from the *face* (where the coal was cut) to the main underground roadway, lads known as *carters* or trammers were taking over and were in charge of the animals. These new developments meant fewer jobs for females. In fact the enquiry into pit work was carried out at a time when women were doing fewer jobs than previously and when, if anything,

Proportions of females to males in the major female employing areas in 1841

District	Male (adults)	Female	Male (between 13–18)	Female	Male (under 13)	Female
Yorkshire	1,000	22	352	36	246	41
Lancashire	1,000	86	352	79	195	27
Midlothians	1,000	333	367	184	131	52
East Lothians	1,000	338	332	296	164	103
West Lothians	1,000	192	289	154	180	109
Stirling	1,000	228	283	129	184	107
Clackmannan	1,000	202	246	213	142	87
Fifeshire	1,000	184	243	109	100	34
Glamorgan	1,000	19	239	12	157	12
Pembrokeshire	1,000	424	366	19	196	19

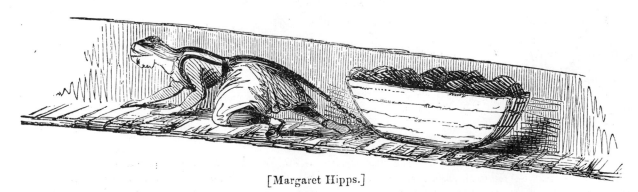

[Margaret Hipps.]

Drawing (pulling tubs) with belt and chain in Scotland

A child's rope harness from about 1840. This would have been placed round the waist.

methods of work were improving slightly. Unlike factory work where skilled workmen were being replaced by machinery and females, the expansion of mining meant new jobs for men.

Women's work was mainly haulage work, that is, transporting coal by a variety of methods. Conditions varied enormously and were affected by geology and the demands of the coalowner. His power was immense. In Scotland, whole collier families were bound to their employers in a system of serfdom until 1799. Here the women not only drew coal but, as the picture shows, performed the extremely demanding job of *coal bearer*. This system had died out in other areas though Pembrokeshire women worked windlasses below and above ground. Several hundred females worked in the small mines of west Wales. Men earned very little there which made female labour

'The Scots Coal Bearer'. Armed with short sticks and a candle held between the teeth the bearer travelled up steep stairways – perhaps 100 feet to the surface with her heavy load. Sometimes she did this for ten hours without a break. One old bearer Isabella Hogg exclaimed 'This is sore, sore work. I wish to God, the first woman who tried to bear coals had broken her back and none would have tried it again'.

especially necessary. There was no other local work for women.

Further east, in the more industrial Welsh areas women also worked at coal and ironstone pits. Although generally boys were *trappers* or door keepers (opening and shutting underground doors for ventilation purposes), there were some girl trappers. Ann Bowcroft had 'kept a door' since the age of five when her father first carried her to work. And there was:

Mary Davies, a very pretty little girl ... fast asleep under a piece of rock near the air-door ... her lamp had gone out for want of oil, and upon waking her, she said the rats or someone had run away with her bread and cheese, so she went to sleep.

Children's Employment Commission, 1842

Conditions in the mines

The enquiry made by the Children's Employment Commission in the early 1840s shows that the average age at which children started mining work was just under nine. This was not unusual in other industries at this time. Most female workers were, however, what we would call teenagers (but were then known as young persons) or they were adults. Many married women did work and some horrifying tales were told of them returning to the mine very soon after having babies. However, most mining women were young and single or were widows of colliers.

Drawing in low, cramped and damp spaces produced stunted bodies and swollen legs. There were dangers of explosions, of roof falls, and accidents with tubs were common. A folk song about a Lancashire colliery woman called Polly Parker tells of the dangers:

By the greatest of dangers each day I'm surrounded;
I hang in the air by a rope or a chain.
The mine may fall in, I may be killed or wounded,
May perish by damp or the fire of the train.
And what would you do if it weren't for our labour?
In wretched starvation your days you would pass,
While we could provide you with life's greatest blessing –
Then do not despise the poor collier lass.

The Collier Lass from 'Poverty Knock'

See page 44 for music and another verse.

As with many early-nineteenth-century industries, there were long hours of work. Collier women might labour for 12 hours non-stop. They also did night work. Colliery surgeons (who could not afford to offend their employers) did not protest about the situation nor, on the whole, did the women themselves. They were not used to complaining and knew little of the sorts of lifestyles that more fortunate people led. For all the work and hardships, the wages seem pitifully low – especially for girls. However, the 1s a day earned by Scots bearers and the 1s 6d which was the average daily rate for adult women drawers were similar to agricultural wages; and the pit brow women who worked above ground a little later did not earn much more. The women and girls wouldn't have considered themselves independent wage earners since they were not paid directly, but through the *hewer* who engaged them. He was usually their father, brother or husband so the women would have seen themselves as contributing to the family income.

With such conditions, it may seem surprising that nothing had been done to improve things in such an old industry. However, very many early Victorians were blissfully ignorant about the lives of those who made possible their industrial greatness. Coalminers' work was, and still is, hidden from view. Colliery communities were mainly in isolated places and, due to the stifling control of the coalowner, were usually very self-sufficient. If people outside pit villages thought of miners at all it was usually with suspicion: a suspicion born of ignorance.

The Commission

So how and why was an enquiry made into the conditions of children working in mines? It was largely the result of what some called 'interference' in the textile trade. The need to control the long hours of work and the ages of those employed in factories had become the centre of a debate which resulted in the 1833 Factory Act forbidding the work of children under nine in textile mills. Some found employment in other industries not yet controlled by law. One man in particular felt an urgent need to extend an umbrella of protection over other industries and so help much greater numbers of children. This was Anthony Ashley Cooper who later became the 7th Earl of Shaftesbury. On 4 August 1840 he outlined his proposals in Parliament. He wanted all children brought 'within the reach of moral and religious education' rather than child employment. The result was a Royal Commission to investigate the conditions of children's employment in a whole range of industries. Four men were to head the first enquiry into mines and collieries. A team of 20 Sub-Commissioners would undertake fieldwork and produce area reports. It was these Sub-Commissioners who were so disturbed by the presence of women in the mines that they decided to include adult women in their reports.

Anthony Ashley Cooper (Lord Shaftesbury)

Victorians believed that a woman's place should be in the home. In middle-class families this was possible (even if not always desired by the young women). However, working-class families were in a very different position and financial necessity rather than choice decided the issue for their womenfolk. The Sub-Commissioners were middle-class and male (not till the 1890s did women head such enquiries) and they were only familiar with their own customs. Their wives and daughters would have been judged by their degree of femininity and the extent to which their behaviour was 'ladylike'. They believed that if women worked in the pits they must be neglecting their homes and families. It was felt that women should remain at home to provide full-time support for their families, especially since there was not yet a national system of education for the young. At this time the working class was becoming organised and political rights were being demanded. 1842 was perhaps the worst year of the century for the economy. It was a time of severe depression and *Chartism*, the first national working-class organisation, was powerful.

The Commission argued that women should be removed from mines in order to protect the state from the growth of an 'ignorant, depraved and dangerous population'. The reports reveal the shock and surprise of gentlemen who were strangers to the working lives of miners. There were criticisms of allowing women to work which failed to appreciate the poverty and lack of decent living standards that faced collier families. The reports had to be produced quickly and the formal questioning of children, sometimes of a very young age, must have been intimidating. Not all the Sub-Commissioners went underground; in fact their reports vary quite considerably in thoroughness.

For those who did enter the mine, it was easy to be shocked by the new world they discovered. They deplored the ignorance of miners, but schools were few and far between and the quality of teaching was generally poor. Lack of religious knowledge was a further shock. Mary Reed went to Sunday school but told the Commission: 'The man in the sky made me but I do not know who he is: never heard of Jesus Christ'. Yet with Sunday as the one day of rest, freedom and light, churches and chapels can't have seemed that appealing. And for female miners the 'day of rest' might be something very different from what it meant for the men. It might be the one time when women could catch up on housework.

The views of the women

The Sub-Commissioners condemned women's work and were especially worried about its effect on their morals. Yet what did the women themselves feel about it? Most of those who expressed views seem to have disliked it intensely. Dinah Bradbury of Lancashire was 18 but asked to be put down as 15 because she thought it might help her chances of leaving. Women and girls emphasised how hard they found the work. In Pembrokeshire they did underground winding which men refused to do because they found it too difficult! One woman there described her work as of 'a sad, tiring sort'. Yet little else was available. Rebecca Hough didn't like her job but was realistic enough to know that where she lived 'there is over many out of place already'. When Mary Ann Watson of Flockton heard that she was likely to lose her job she was so 'overpowered with fear' that she could not continue talking. For widows, pit work might be the only way of holding on to a colliery house.

The diarist Munby later talked to some women who had formerly worked in the mines. He believed in such work (unlike most of his

An extract from 'Boompin' Nell' by Munby. Ellen Meggison 'is one of my oldest friends' said Munby.

Sir, you Know what I can do: and I wish I was at it ageean –
With a tub o' coal behind me, an my own owd belt an cheean!
Eh, what a shame it is, as they treats us wenches so!
Never with your leave or by your leave, they tell'd us all to go;
They've took the bread clean oot on oor mooths, aye, every mother an maid,
An all for to pleasure the menfolk, as wants to steal oor trade!
Well, if it's hard an mucky, who knows that better nor me?
But I liked it, an it was my living – an so it had ought to be:
Surely, a wench mun choose her work! An as for the dirt you know
I was hardly blacker, down i' the pit, nor I are as you see me now.
Couldn't I work theer ageean, Sir? I'd go as snug as I can;

contemporaries) and he felt that most women had not wanted to stop. He recalled the enthusiasm of one Wigan woman who slapped her thigh for emphasis and said: 'Ah'd give em a footnat's work for nothing if tha'd nobbut let m'a''. In his poem 'Boompin' Nell' (based on a real pit woman called Ellen Meggison) he summed up what seem to have been his own feelings.

Munby also met Ann Eggley, a Yorkshire lass who had been interviewed for the Children's Employment Commission when she was eighteen. At that time she had said that her work was far too hard and that she was very tired at night. Fourteen years later, married with three children, she was asked by Munby whether the 1842 ban was a good thing. Her answer was that 'It was for some things but not for others' and she added:

'The girls never behaved badly. The work was hard but not for me. I did not dislike it and if I was not married I'd like to work in the pit again. I'd like it better than anything else – yes, much better'.

Was memory being kind to her? Perhaps the truth lies somewhere between the Commission's exaggeration of evils and Munby's romantic views. One thing, though is certain. It *was* a case of 'never with your leave or by your leave'; the women who worked below ground had the decision about their futures made for them.

How a contemporary paper exaggerated the original drawing of Ann and Will

Out of the mine

Ashley's determination and powerful speeches helped to ensure the success of the Mines bill. His strongest words were reserved for the evils of women's pit work. Their removal from work in the mine was made the first demand of the bill, even though the original idea had been merely to investigate children's employment. Newspaper reports show us how the Commission had shocked the public. Comparisons were made with black slaves (in 1833 Britain had abolished slavery in her colonies). For the first time a Parliamentary report included illustrations. Some were reproduced in newspapers and even exaggerated to produce a more sensational story. Compare this picture of Ann Ambler

and Will Dyson with the original on page 4. Newspapers were now big business and competing for a growing readership. Rival papers saw stories of mining women as possible 'scoops' and, whatever their political views, they condemned the work. Ashley also received many petitions begging for females to be banned from the mines.

He was delighted with the impact of his two-hour speech attacking the work. You could have heard a pin drop in the House of Commons, so attentively did the MPs listen. The support was tremendous and cut right across the political parties. The House of Lords proved more tricky. Coalowners such as the Marquis of Londonderry were not prepared to support a bill which threatened their influence, would ban boys under ten as well as women and girls and would appoint people to keep an eye on how collieries were run.

However the bill did succeed and it became law on 10 August 1842. Within three months all females under 18 had to leave underground work. The rest had to go before 1 March 1843. This was the first time that adult females had been legally excluded from a particular employment, though just over two years later a new Factory Act restricted the hours that women could work. These moves reflected wider attitudes towards women. Lacking political and many legal rights they were felt to be, like children, in need of protection. This process was, as we shall see, to develop still further later in the century.

The results

If the law-makers believed that the women could simply be taken out of the pits and remain at home without any problems, then they were in for a shock. It was one thing to pass a law, but quite another to enforce it. Decisions made in London could not easily or rapidly be put into practice elsewhere and the coalowners themselves acted as a powerful force against change. Raising the height of roadways to enable ponies to replace females and boys cost money. It was cheaper, simpler and more convenient for all concerned simply to turn a blind eye to the law. It wasn't difficult since only one person,
H. S. Tremenheere, was appointed to enforce it in the country's 2,000 collieries! He wrote yearly progress reports and trusted in gradual improvement over time.

There was little alternative work available at a time of such depression and mining areas were especially isolated. Women were likely to find themselves in competition with each other for what few jobs might exist and, given peoples' opinions of miners they didn't feel they stood much chance in any competition. The law was intended to encourage women to stay at home and look after their families. Yet the need for money, quite often to help elderly or disabled relatives, as well as themselves, was the reason why they were doing the work in

the first place! Compensation was not provided, nor was advice at hand despite all the fine, caring words that had been uttered when the report first came out. In 1845 Tremenheere estimated that out of 2,400 female miners, only 200 had found other work. There was a small amount of domestic service, a little seasonal work in the fields and the occasional opening in local industries, but basically there were too many people after too few jobs.

Very few coalowners seem to have accepted responsibility for their workforce. Lord and Lady Francis Egerton at Worsley, Lancashire, were amongst the few exceptions. They began phasing out women's work at the pits before the law was passed and did it gradually so that there were not large numbers searching for work at the same time. They started the Walkden Moor Servants School to train former pit girls for domestic service and found some women light agricultural work on the estate. Most impressive (and exceptional) was their allowance scheme which paid 1s a week to parents for a year to compensate for the loss of daughters' earnings until they got a job or stopped attending school. Adult women miners also got some payment. Though small, it must have been a valuable help in adjusting. This early form of redundancy payment was a far cry from the lack of concern shown by the overwhelming number of coalowners.

Many female miners simply ignored the ban on their work. There seemed little choice but to continue the job they knew, even if they hated it and were breaking the law. Tremenheere reported cases of evasion but his employer, the Home Office, was reluctant to spend money on following up cases. It was difficult to prove that females were working underground and coalowners could easily afford to pay the small fines if the women were caught. Tremenheere engaged a few informers though had difficulty finding recruits. In Wigan alone in 1845 at least 200 women were known to be breaking the law.

Munby met one woman who started work underground for the *first* time in 1848 and stayed there for about eighteen months. Others worked illegally in the 1850s. One, with a relative to support, told how she was paid 3s less per week than when her work was legal. Yet for her, as for others, such work was the lesser of two evils, deception or destitution. As late as 1866 an accident revealed women (including one who was pregnant) working in a pit in south Wales, engaged cheaply by *sub-contractors*.

Gradually the numbers declined. The male miners played a part in this. Their first national union, the Miners' Association, was formed in 1842 and, seeking better conditions for the industry, its members felt that mining was not suitable for women. In 1841 Barnsley colliers had declared that 'the employment of girls in pits is highly injurious to their morals', deploring 'this scandalous practice'. The development of ideas about what was or wasn't fit work for women was encouraging them to argue that the womenfolk should be as entitled to stay at home as their employers' wives. Yet not all miners spoke against women's work. Those who depended upon jobs traditionally done by the females in their families found themselves in a difficult position. However, at the official level the all-male union was increasingly critical of this form of female employment and was arguing that, instead men should be earning a decent enough wage to support the whole family so that the women would not need to work.

Also, jobs on the surface were beginning to expand and in some cases women coalminers were able to get work above ground. This was still legal though it annoyed the miners' union which felt that men should do these jobs. It was complicated because the coalowners tended to favour women workers, largely because they could pay them far less than men. They were also not in unions and were thought to be less likely to stir up trouble or strike. Some owners even laid off surface men and replaced them with women, arguing that men could find other jobs more easily than women. The miners resented this and saw the women as cheap labour.

So, thought Margaret Park, this helps explain why many of the miners are not supporting the pit women today. And with these thoughts, she hurried off to her meeting, accompanied by her friend the Reverend Harry Mitchell.

Before seeing how Margaret fared, we will look more closely at these pit brow lasses who interested her and try to picture their daily lives.

Clackmannan, June 10th, 1844

My Lord,

being on a visit to this part of Scotland I find that the act for the prevention of females working in pits is daily and openly violated and set at defiance! The Clackmannan Coal Company trading under the name of Wilson & co, employ upwards of one hundred females in their coal works in this Neighbourhood and that without the least attempt at concealment!

I am also prepared to prove that women are employed in the coal pits in other parts of Scotland — many at the Duke of Hamilton's collieries at Redding near Falkirk, in fact My Lord your humane act so far as Scotland is concerned is a dead letter! — I sincerely hope your Lordship will exert yourself to see the act carried out, and to prevent the law being thus violated with impunity, . . .

I am My Lord, your Lordships obedient humble servant,
William Daniells

Rt Hon'l Lord Ashley

Part of a letter from William Daniells, Secretary of the Scottish miners to Ashley, complaining that part of the 1842 Act is being ignored:

3 Above ground – the pit lass

Names and numbers

The pit brow lass or lassie was the girl or woman who worked above ground at coal mines. This is a Lancashire term but writers tended to use it when referring to pit women generally. This was probably because a greater number of women worked at mines in this area than anywhere else in Britain. In 1886 when the future of the women's work was being keenly debated by Margaret Park and others, almost 40 per cent of the total number of women pit workers were employed in west Lancashire, mainly around the towns of Wigan and St Helens. There were also some lesser known terms: in Cumberland the women pit workers were called screen lasses, in the Black Country they were pit bank wenches, in Scotland pit head workers and in Wales where they worked at iron mines, they were known as tip girls.

It is difficult to know exactly how many females were employed in the nineteenth century since many moved from job to job or worked only for a short time, generally leaving when they married or had a child. Not until 1874 are the figures even partially reliable. From this date we can see who was working at a particular date from the reports of the Inspectors of Mines. As you can see from the table the numbers fell from just under 7,000 in that year to just over 4,000 by 1886. It was in 1886 that a serious attempt was made to stop the women working.

Most of the women were single and many were quite young, though they had to be over ten. Some collieries forbade married women to work. Gradually laws were passed which kept young people in school for longer periods. For example, the Education Act of 1880 made school attendance compulsory for those aged between five and ten, though children under 14 could work providing they could prove that they had attended a school or had reached some level of educational achievement. In 1887 the starting age was raised to 12. Some girls

Number of surface females in different districts in 1886

N. Wales	61
S. Wales	835
W. Scotland	41
E. Scotland	576
Yorkshire	5
N. Staffs, Cheshire, Shropshire	319
S. Staffs, Worcs.	237
Northumberland, Durham, Cumberland	398*
N. and E. Lancs	317
W. Lancs	1,321

* All but 3 were in Cumberland.

Numbers of surface females at coal, iron, shale and clay mines

Year	Females	Total surface labour force
1874	6,899	110,218
1881	4,715	96,090
1887	4,183	97,737
1890	4,206	106,421
1900	4,808	155,829

worked as 'half-timers', spending part of the day at a school and the rest at work. One Wigan girl who began in this way at the age of $12\frac{1}{2}$ was so small that the manager had to tell her to bring two bricks to stand on in order to reach the *picking belts*.

What exactly did these girls and women do? The answer is that they performed a wide range of jobs which helped prepare the coal to be sold. The demands and pace of the work and the daily duties could vary quite considerably. In the summer, for example, they were not usually as busy as in the winter months, when there was a greater demand for coal. Perhaps the best way of illustrating the variety of work and the effect it had on peoples' lives is to look at it through the eyes of the pit women. To do this we shall follow a weekend in the life of Jane Brown. She was a real pit lass who worked at Wigan collieries in the 1860s. We know quite a lot about her and her family because of the diaries, notebooks, sketches and poetry of Arthur Munby.

Munby called Wigan 'The picturesque headquarters of rough female labour' and he visited Jane and her family a number of times. We can discover further information about her by looking at the population census for 1861 which gives details of the Brown family. We can also find out about her home town by looking at sources such as the local newspaper, the *Wigan Observer*.

Jane's weekend

It is four o'clock on a September morning and although it is a Saturday, Jane Brown has to get up and go to work. The year is 1866 and Jane is almost 22. She lives with her family in a stone cottage in the middle of a neat row of houses at New Springs near Wigan and she has to walk two miles daily to her work at the pit. She gets up quietly. There are only two bedrooms and Jane has to share a bed with her baby and one of her sisters. In the other bed her elder sister Lizzie and her child are fast asleep with another sister Maria. Lizzie will soon have to stir. Jane's parents and a 12-year-old sister sleep in one bed in the other bedroom while her two brothers share the other bed. One of them is finishing his night shift at the pit so his brother has the bed to himself.

Jane puts on her blue shirt, a waistcoat and the famous Wigan trousers and clogs. By late-twentieth-century standards she would be considered quite fashionably dressed, but Victorians do not consider trousers to be a decent form of clothing for women. Jane knows, however, that although women in other mining areas do not wear them, trousers are warm and very practical for her kind of work. She quickly braids her long golden hair and covers it with a scarf. She needs to do this as coal dust gets everywhere. At 5 feet 4 inches (1.63 m) she is shorter than a lot of collier

women but she makes up for her lack of height with her strong, square shoulders. Jane washes quickly out in the yard though she will never really get rid of the layer of black coal dust that is ingrained in her skin. Chewing a chunk of bread she grabs her snack or 'baggin', prepared by her mother the night before. Lizzie appears and they set off together, calling next door for another girl who works with them. They wear large jackets, men's cast-offs, to keep them warm.

Lizzie is two years older than Jane and used to work at a cotton mill. She lost her job because of the acute shortage of cotton (sometimes called the cotton famine), due to the American Civil War of 1861 to 1865. These had been tough years for Wigan's cotton workers, most of whom are women. By mid-1862 eighteen mills had been closed and others were not working full-time. Close to a quarter of the population of Wigan were out of work or unable to do a proper week's work.

Jane Brown ('Jaan Brahn' is Munby's spelling) in her working clothes

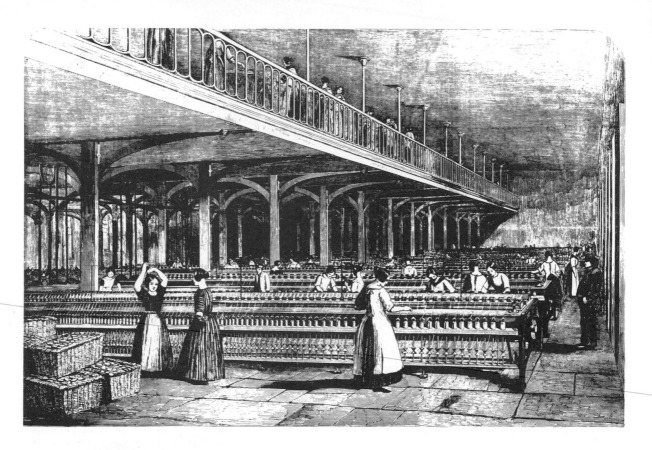

A Lancashire cotton mill

Lizzie would have been extremely lucky to have remained in employment. Only two mills worked full-time and they only provided work for about 350 people. Even Jane had suffered because the coalowners had soon reduced wages in mining due to the reduced demand for fuel. Lizzie had been fortunate. Having a sister working at the colliery helped and she was eventually able to get a job with Jane at the Ince Hall Coal and *Cannel* Company. Lizzie prefers mill work as it is much cleaner, though she does admit that the open air in which she now works is bracing and better for her than the dusty, confined atmosphere of the mill. In fact Wigan doctors sometimes advise millworkers to go to the pit brow to improve their health!

The Browns are a mining family. Not only is the father, Henry Brown, a miner of many years experience but his wife Alice, now 53, once worked underground, helping to transport coal in the days before the work was banned for women. The oldest son George is in

his late twenties and is a seasoned collier like his father. The younger brother is already working at the pit. The two youngest daughters are not yet working though 12-year-old Ann Brown has recently started as a pit lass.

On this autumn morning Jane and Lizzie arrive at work on time. Their workday begins at 6 a.m. and ends at 5 p.m. though today will be easier than some as they will finish early. It is 'Reckoning day' – pay day. This takes place every other Saturday between 3 p.m. and 4 p.m. and the pit lasses, along with the miners, collect their wages. The Ince Hall Company is one of the largest of the Wigan coal companies.

The sisters work at Bottom Place pit, or Patricroft as it is known. This is the most accessible pit in the Wigan area, close to the railway line and to the centre of the town. Curious strangers and newspaper reporters who want to find out about pit lasses come here. At least they, unlike some of the critics,

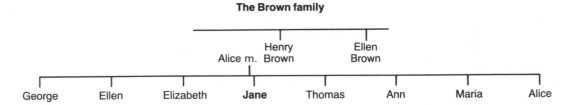

The Brown family

Alice m. Henry Brown · Ellen Brown

George · Ellen · Elizabeth · **Jane** · Thomas · Ann · Maria · Alice

All the members of the family shown above worked at some time in coal mining as did a number of Henry and Alice's grandchildren.

No. of Schedule	Road, Street, &c., and No. or Name of House	Houses In-habited	Houses Un-inhabited (U.), or Building (B.)	Name and Surname of each Person	Relation to Head of Family	Condition	Age of Males	Age of Females	Rank, Profession, or Occupation	Where Born	Whether Blind, or Deaf and-Dumb
18	New Springs			Richard Broomhead	Son		10		Scholar	Lancash. Ince	
				John do	Son		8		do	do do	
				Betsy do	Daur			5	do	do do	
				Margaret do	Daur			10m		do Haigh	
				Betsy Bentham	Mother in law			60	Retired Grocer	Northumberland Newcastle on Tyne	
19	New Springs	1		William Gibson	Head	Mar	41		Foreman at Colliery	Lancash. Aspull	
				Jane do	Wife	Mar		41		do Haigh	
				Ellen do	Daur	Un		17	Cotton weaver	do Haigh	
				Jane do	Daur			8	Scholar	do Aspull	
				Noah do	Son		6		do	do do	
				Alice do	Daur			1		do Haigh	
20	New Springs	1		Henry Brown	Head	Mar	52		Coal miner	do do	
				Alice do	Wife	Mar		47		do Upholland	
				George do	Son	Un	22		Coal miner	do Haigh	
				Elizabeth do	Daur	Un		19	Cotton weaver	do do	
				Jane do	Daur	Un		17	Colliery labourer	do do	
				Ann do	Daur			9	Scholar	do do	
				Maria do	Daur			7	do	do do	
				Alice do	Daur			3		do do	
				Mary do	Grand Daur			1m		do do	
				Thomas do	Son	Un	15		Drawer in Coal mine	do do	
21	New Springs	1		Elizabeth Melling	Head	W		58	Housekeeper	do do	
				Thomas do	Son	Un	35		Coal miner	do Aspull	
				Samuel do	do	Un	24		do	do Haigh	
				Alice do	Daur	Un		17	Reeler in Cotton mill	do Aspull	
	Total of Houses... 3				Total of Males and Females...		9	16			

The census of 1861 showing the Brown family

are able to see at first hand the nature of the work. They can observe for themselves that the sifting, sorting and transporting of coal is performed in conditions preferable to those which women had previously faced below ground. However, the colliery management is worried that its surface workers are being distracted by the attention being paid to them by visitors. So it has recently forbidden strangers to wander around the pit top. It has also recently stopped most women working on the brow itself where the tubs of coal are unloaded. Munby considers this 'an absurd innovation'. Previously women had helped to unload the tubs from the mouth of the pit after they had come up the cage. They were assisted by men. They used also to push tubs along the pit top to be tipped into the *screens* below.

Although many collieries try not to pay too much attention to criticisms about women pit

Unloading at the pit top

(*Left*) *Tipping and screeening*

workers, the Ince Hall pits are less isolated than most and therefore they are quite sensitive to publicity. Women continue to work at the brow at many other pits and Jane has a friend who operates the *tippler* at one colliery.

Increasingly however, the main job for women is that of sorting coal. In order to separate the different sizes of coal, screens or bars set at a fixed distance from one another are used. The women's task is to separate the coal from the dirt and other impurities. In some parts of the country (for example, the North-East), elderly or disabled miners or young lads do this work, standing in rows in front of the coal. At Ince Hall they have a simple type of screen which, unlike the later ones, is stationary and it is the girls and women who have to move around them. They sometimes use long rakes to separate the coal. The pit manager, George Gilroy had described their work in June when he gave evidence to a

House of Commons Committee investigating mining:

Coals run over screen bars: the dust and small coal fall through those bars, and the riddled (sieved) coal remains on the top: the duty of the women is to pick the dirt, the shale, and stone, and refuse out of the coal.

The screens at Ince Hall are fairly new and the job of sorting coal is popular as it is under cover. Some collieries do not yet have screens and still rely on riddling or sieving by hand. You can see the *riddles* in the photograph. One Wigan miner explained to the mining committee that the women's main tasks were riddling and wheeling tubs to wagons or barges. Ince Hall is close to the Leeds and Liverpool canal and Lizzie fills trucks while

Jane works down by the canal. Jane thrutches (pushes) and manoeuvres heavy tubs of coal. She also helps to dig coal and load it. She used to work at the Rose Bridge colliery but she left when she had her baby.

Most women tend to move on after a few years – there is plenty of choice with so many pits being developed in the area. It's possible to work at eight or ten different ones without needing to move house. Although the majority of young women of Jane's age work at the mill when times are good, colliery work is expanding for women. Women pit brow workers now make up over 40 per cent of those women workers who are not employed at the local mills. Over 500 pit women work in the area around Wigan and the Ince Hall pits

Pit lasses with riddles

Filling trucks

employ about 80 of them. The textile women, however, are in the majority, and see themselves as superior to the pit lasses especially since weaving and spinning are skilled jobs and can command quite good wages. It doesn't help that the pit girls and women are usually seen when they are filthy dirty. Munby is struck by the 'thundering of coals' and the 'whirling of dense black clouds' when he visits Jane at work, and, as yet, there is no such thing as pithead baths.

Jane needs to be strong and healthy to do her work. Using his own spelling to suggest Jane's dialect, Munby records her words in his diary: 'Aye, they all say as ahm strong enough to be a mon'. Jane had found it hard, demanding work when she first started pushing tubs but her mother had told her that it was child's play compared to what she had done in the mine when she was tiny! Also, Jane soon discovered that there is a knack to doing it, a

way of using her body which distributes the impact and weight evenly; even though nobody ever taught her what to do, she soon picked it up. Now she works rapidly until her first brief break at eight o'clock. She then grabs a quick bite. Normally she has a midday meal in the cabin where she rests with the other girls and women, joking with them as she gobbles down a meat pasty. Today being Saturday there won't be another break. The 'gaffer' (the man in charge of them) keeps an eye on the lasses. Very occasionally Mr Gilroy the manager comes round and several times he has brought with him the Senior Partner in the firm, John Lancaster.

Although Jane and her mates like a chat, they always keep a careful eye on their work. They need to. A short while ago, a friend, Sarah Broadhurst aged 29, had been killed at another local pit. She had been coupling wagons (linking railway wagons together) on

20

Date.	No. of Accidents.	Name of Colliery.	Where situate.	Owner's or Agent's Name.	Persons killed.	Occupation.	Age.	Cause of Death, and Remarks.	Explosions.	Falls of Roof.	In Shafts.	Miscellaneous.	Above ground.
								Brought forward -	9	26	17	14	10
1865. Sept. 9	67	Hanmer - -	Mostyn, Holywell	Eyton and Elliot -	Thomas Roberts -	Bank laborer	60	From injuries by coal trucks on the surface railway.	-	-	-	-	1
	68	Kirkless Hall -	Kirkless, Wigan	Kirkless Hall Coal and Iron Company.	Sarah Broadhurst -	Coaldresser	29	Ditto ditto -	-	-	-	-	1
„ 12	69	California -	Aspull, Wigan -	Ditto - - -	E. Anderton -	Colliers -	-	The rope breaking by slipping off the drum as the deceased were ascending the pit. It was a conical or compensating drum without groves.	-	-	1	-	-
		Ditto -	Ditto - -	Ditto - - -	John Dunn -		-		-	-	1	-	-
		Ditto -	Ditto - -	Ditto - - -	J. Ramsdale -		-		-	-	1	-	-
		Ditto -	Ditto - -	Ditto - - -	G. Ingram -		-		-	-	1	-	-
		Ditto -	Ditto - -	Ditto - - -	R. Fletcher -		-		-	-	1	-	-
		Ditto -	Ditto - -	Ditto - - -	W. Bradshaw -		-		-	-	1	-	-
		Ditto -	Ditto - -	Ditto - - -	Robert Ealock -		-		-	-	1	-	-
		Ditto -	Ditto - -	Ditto - - -	John Holland -		-		-	-	1	-	-
„ 12	70	Brynmally -	Wrexham -	Thomas Clayton - -	Wm. Jones -	Collier -	19	Fall of coal at a slip in Brassey mine	-	1	-	-	-
„ 14	71	Sankey Brook -	St. Helen's -	Sankey Brook Coal Compy.	James Kay -	Drawer -	17	Fall of coal Little Delf mine -	-	1	-	-	-
„ 14	72	Garswood Park -	Ditto -	David Bromilow & Co. -	Thomas Stockley -	Collier -	42	Fall of roof - - - -	-	1	-	-	-
„ 15	73	Tryddyn -	Mold -	Flintshire Oil & Cannel Co.	Ellis Roberts -	Banksman -	38	Falling into the pit from the surface	-	-	1	-	-
„ 20	74	Newton -	Wigan -	Lamb and Moore -	John Murray -	Hooker-on -	16	Fall of coal off an ascending tub -	-	-	1	-	-
„ 21	75	Heskin -	Chorley -	Thomas Whaley -	Joseph Watson -	Ditto -	51	The signal hammer got loose and fell upon from the top of the pit.	-	-	1	-	-
Oct. 7	76	Park Lane -	Ashton, Wigan -	Mercer and Evans -	P. Wilkinson -	Banksman -	46	Deceased fell off the coal screen on the pit bank.	-	-	-	-	1
„ 11	77	White Moss -	Blaquegate, Ormskirk.	Lord Skelmersdale -	Samuel Griffiths -	Sinker -	38	Deceased fell out of the bucket into some water in a sinking pit.	-	-	1	-	-
„ 16	78	Gidlow Lane -	Standish, Wigan	The Kirkless Hall Coal and Iron Company	Thomas Topping -	Ditto -	50	In this case death was caused by an iron drill falling off the ascending bucket.	-	-	1	-	-
„ 17	79	Ewloe Hall -	Buckley, Mold -	Ewloe Hall Coal Compy. -	Peter Davidson -	Collier -	40	Fall of roof - - - -	-	1	-	-	-
„ 20	80	Gardden Lodge -	Ruabon, Denbighshire.	Gardden Lodge Colliery Company.	Edward Griffiths -	Ditto -	47	By the rope breaking - - -	-	-	1	-	-
„ „	81	Ince Hall -	Ince, Wigan -	Ince Hall Coal & Cannel Company.	James Anderton -	Ditto -	40	Fall of roof - - - -	-	1	-	-	-
								Carried forward -	9	31	31	14	13

An Inspector's Report showing Sarah's accident

the colliery line and was crushed between the buffers. At the Inquest a verdict of 'Accidental death' was recorded. A number of such gruesome deaths have been recorded and many pits, especially the small ones which do not have much money invested in them, lack decent safety precautions. The Inspector is rarely seen, though he has such a big area to cover that it is not really surprising. He always warns the manager when he is about to make a visit so it is quite easy for some employers to ignore safety conditions most of the time. Attention is anyway largely focused on the work underground and the need to prevent accidents there. Some surface jobs are, however, also potentially lethal, especially work on the colliery line. As well as moving wagons, women oil and grease them and there are some pointswomen. Of course these jobs are not just dangerous for women, they are a hazard for anybody doing them. It is interesting though to note that the accidents which involve women receive rather more newspaper publicity than those which befall male surface workers. This provides a further opportunity for people to attack the work as unsuitable for women.

As two o'clock approaches, the pit lasses begin to clear up. They are usually the last to leave their shift because they still have to handle the coal after the men have sent the last load up. Jane and her friends go to collect their 'brass' (money). On the way they are joined by the eccentric Munby who looks rather out of place in his immaculate suit and hat. The pit women have nicknamed him 'the Inspector' as he always seems to be writing things down. They can't really see what he finds to write about and can't help thinking that life in London must be much more exciting than working at the pit all day. They find him a curious yet likeable person though they sometimes tease him a bit about getting a 'missus'. They feel, however, that they need to be a bit careful about what they say as he is a gentleman. One good thing is that he quite often gives them 6d or perhaps even 1s after chatting to them for a while.

On the way to Middle Place pit where the wages are paid out, the group pass the Crown Inn. Munby offers Jane and her workmates, Mary Atherton and Ann Prescot, a beer. They willingly accept as pit work is tiring and it makes them thirsty. Jane sees her uncle inside

Munby's sketch of a lady and an 'oiler'

having a drink and he buys her some bread and cheese and her favourite dish, a saucer of boiled pickled peas. Munby tries it but doesn't like the bitter taste even though the landlord assures him that he sells a vast quantity of the dish every Saturday. Ann chooses a piece of bacon instead. She is glad of the company. Her parents have recently left by railway to live in Staffordshire and she is missing her sister who has joined them in the hope of finding a job at an ironstone pit there. Ann who is 21 has stayed behind to keep house for her brother who also works for John Lancaster.

Many pit women look after relatives, a large number of whom are dependent upon their help and money. Some have elderly fathers disabled by coaldust and unable to work because of the state of their lungs. And there are some like Jane who have illegitimate children. Wigan has the highest rate of illegitimacy in Lancashire and although most women eventually marry the father of their children, they do not necessarily do so straightaway, nor feel that they should do so. The outsider Munby has difficulty in

understanding such customs. He notes in his diary that he has 'spoken roundly' to Lizzie and Jane. They must have been puzzled by his concern. He says 'They both took my words very quietly admitting it was a bad job but not seeing any disgrace in it'. Jane feels that she is not yet ready to marry her sweetheart, but he does give her 2s weekly towards the cost of keeping her baby Mary.

The other pit woman, Mary Atherton is a lot older. She was once a weaver but is now widowed and working at the colliery in order to keep on the house which is owned by the company and was first rented when her collier husband was alive. Of the 78 pit women working at Ince Hall only 13 are married and 5 are widows. Some widows take in lodgers to make a little more money. Others take on some extra work such as washing clothes. Much depends on whether they have children at home who are of an age when they can earn money. If they do not and there are little ones at home, then it can be very hard to make ends meet. The Ince Hall company does have a welfare scheme to which women can belong, but it doesn't go far in providing funds. The women always earn much less than a man. Even the elderly or disabled male miners (who tend to work more slowly than the young women) still earn twice their wages.

Jane is now earning 2s a day. Over the last three years the daily rate for the pit women has gone up by 2d. Munby knows one woman who went with her friends to see about increasing the amount when wages stood at 1s 10d;

Me and soom oother women went to 't owaerseer an' wa tell'd him hoo things was advanced, and t' men was getting moor, an' waat'd him for two shillin'. Well, he'd see aboot it, he said; an't next Saturday, t' reckonin' was maad aht for t'wenches to ha' two shillin.

However Jane's friend Ellen Fairhurst has been earning 2s for some time. She also works at Ince Hall at the same pit but she is a washer of the small coal or slack. Clean small coal is needed for coke ovens and Lancashire leads the way in installing coal-washing plants. They are the forerunners of the twentieth-century

washeries and provide a more effective way of cleaning small coal than hand picking. Coal and dirt are placed in troughs of water and Ellen and another girl use rakes to agitate the coal and move it around. These slackwashers consider themselves privileged as they work under cover, by themselves; they remain cleaner than all the others and they earn a few extra pennies.

The women line up as pay-time approaches. The men get paid first. At last it's Jane's turn. The clerk calls out her name and two weeks' wages, wrapped in paper, are paid out. Jane, like other colliery workers, both sons and daughters, hands over her wages to her mother. A small amount goes to the Sick and Burial society and has already been deducted – women pay half the subscription paid by the men. Her mother receives the wage as she is the one who is expected to administer and juggle the family's wages so that they can pay all the bills. Jane gets back 6d as pocket money. She has been trying to save but recently all her money was spent in

Pay time

Bathing time in a mining home

Colliers' houses in Wigan.

This is the street where Jane and her family lived.

one go – she paid the large sum of 4s 6d for a blue bonnet for little Mary: 'The prettiest baby in England', she tells Munby.

Jane now walks home. She takes her time as Saturday night is cleaning night and she knows that once indoors she won't have a chance to get out again. Fridays are her favourite evenings because then she joins all her friends at the weekly Wigan market. Today however she must help in the house. First she has her tea, even before she washes off the coal dust, and then she spends some time with her baby. It's a bustling house with people coming and going. Neighbours are in and out all day long and there is a blazing, welcoming fire made possible because of the cheap coal allowed to colliers, one of the few advantages of the job. This means that there is no excuse for Jane not to do the scrubbing properly as there is plenty of hot water. She also has to do her share of mending. She finds the material of her father's trousers so tough that only by first putting the needle through a bar of soap can she hope to get it into the cloth. This is one of the many tips she has picked up over the years. Meanwhile Mrs Brown, a very plump woman dressed all in black, is busy baking for the

Aunt Ellen: according to Munby 'Jane behaved very kindly to her'.

family. Recently there has been another addition to the household: an aunt, whose father (Jane's grandfather) has just died. Like many mining families the Browns are a close family used to taking care of relatives in times of crisis. They are fortunate because Aunt Ellen brings with her a small wage. She is a bricksetter at the nearby Pigeon pit. She chips mortar off old bricks and stacks them in barrows. She does much of this sitting down as she was crippled in an underground pit accident. She is 46 and single but Munby thinks she looks ten years younger.

Jane goes to bed before nine o'clock. Sunday is her one day of rest. She says she likes then to 'stop a' whoam and laak (play) abaht'. Several years earlier she had started to learn to read at the 'Methody' (*Methodist* Sunday school). She had enjoyed this and still sometimes tries to pick her way through some of the Penny Romances which are very popular in Wigan. Not surprisingly, the educational standards of Jane and her friends are not very high. If any opportunity arises for schooling within families it is always the boys who are given the first chance. A survey at Jane's colliery in 1853 had revealed that out of 49 pit women, only 12 could read and one sign her name. No national system of *elementary education* is yet in existence and Jane and many parents of pit lasses cannot really see how school can equip them for the kind of lives they feel they are more-or-less bound to lead. A number of the women do, however, go to religious services and Sunday school. The Rector of Wigan estimates that about half of the 80 girls and women who attend his weekly Bible classes come from the collieries. As well as the Church of England and Nonconformist denominations such as the Methodists, Wigan has a large number of Catholics, many of whom are Irish women working at the mills. Yet Wigan's total church attendance figures are low, even compared with other towns. In a Census of religion taken in 1851 less than 30 per cent of Wigan's population were recorded as going to a religious service on the day the numbers were counted. From an early age girls are expected to help at home, not just with

Nan Morgan in the photographer's studio in 1865

Jane in her Sunday best

housework but with looking after younger brothers and sisters. For many of Wigan's female population there is little time to attend religious services, nor is there the opportunity or money for many to attend school.

Jane is no longer able to go to Sunday school as she has to spend her time with her baby. Her mother looks after her during the week, but on Sundays Jane dresses in her best clothes (her one dress) and takes the baby out for a walk with her sweetheart. This is the one day when she does not wear trousers. As Munby comments in his diary, 'really a collier girl hardly ever wears women's clothing except on Sundays'. Recently Jane and all the other

Ince Hall women were photographed wearing their Sunday dresses by a local photographer, Mr Cooper. This was so that the company could hand round pictures when the manager gave evidence to the mining committee and so show that the women were not made unfeminine by such work. The Wigan photographers, Cooper, Little, Dugdale, Wragg, Millard and Craig regularly take pictures of the women. They make them look somewhat curious as they usually wear their pit clothes and have to pose against rather romantic studio settings, some of which look more like the Swiss Alps than Wigan! Pictures such as the one of a Welsh pit girl, Nan

26

Morgan who now works in Wigan, are displayed in the streets and shop windows and sell in their dozens. Commercial travellers and others buy them as 'curiosities'. No doubt the trousers add to their fascination. Jane's friend Sarah Fairhurst (sister of Ellen the slackwasher) has told Munby that she was not happy having her picture taken by the company. She doesn't like being 'draw'd aht i'me pi-claas' for fear of being exhibited in Cooper's window.

Looking back today it is tempting for us to conclude that pit women such as the Fairhurst and Brown sisters became objects of curiosity for people who were often far removed from the pit themselves and who would have been in positions to resist much more strongly than the pit girls could, any examination of their own lives. Some people argued that the work was degrading and unwomanly and attacked it, just as the very different work below ground had been attacked in 1842. Others saw the pit brow lass as a perfect demonstration of women's strength and ability.

Yet Jane doesn't see it like any of these people. For her, it is a hard, tiring and demanding job that has to be done. It pays little, yet it provides her with good friends and keeps her out of an overcrowded house. Yet, although she falls asleep on Sunday night hoping that the morning won't come too quickly, she most certainly would not agree with those who want to take her job away from her.

4 The right to work

Let us leave Jane undisturbed, enjoying her rest before her long day begins again and move forward in time again to the mid-1880s. This is when serious attempts are being made to ban women like Jane from their work at the pit brow. This work is changing. The *picking belts* at the foot of the screens are where most women now work. The screens have become more sophisticated with different travelling belts attached for the different sizes of coal. Some belts are very long. They move slowly and the women pick out perhaps as much as a ton of dirt daily. As you can see from the picture it involves a lot of bending. It is noisy too with the screens working continuously; Wigan women nickname them 'shakers'. In Cumberland where women work at screen tables instead of belts, one table is nicknamed 'Jane Ann' after a particularly experienced screen lass.

Jane has married the father of her baby and she no longer works at the pit. Her daughter Mary does instead. She pushes tubs of coal at the Alexandra pit with her cousin Alice Heywood. Compare the picture of Alice with the formal studio photographs in the last chapter and see how much more relaxed this girl looks. Alice is standing quite naturally and even has a smile on her face! Lizzie's daughter also works with them. One person has however got right away from the pit. Jane's brother is now the proud owner of a butcher's shop in the busy centre of Wigan. As you can see from the table, the town has grown dramatically.

Picking belts

Young Alice Heywood in 1887

Wigan, County Borough population

1841	25,517
1861	37,658
1881	48,194

Just over half the population is female. Wigan has both a high birth-rate and a large number of immigrants. Many of the latter are Irish girls and women who are spinners in the mills. The number of pit lasses has increased, with over 1,300 working in the Wigan and St Helens area by the 1880s.

The old market town has become a busy industrial borough. For centuries Wigan has boasted its own Mayor and Council. The present Mayor is Henry Park, Margaret's husband. He is the longest serving Mayor in Wigan's history, having first held office in 1882. But we are more concered with his wife, since she is the one who organises the campaign to keep pit lasses such as young Alice and Mary in work. Let us look more closely at Margaret's life.

Margaret Richmond was born in Liverpool in 1835, the eldest daughter in her family. For a middle-class girl life was restricted. Unlike Jane and her friends, she did not have to go to

Part of central Wigan

29

work at an early age to bring home some income for the family. In fact the employment of young ladies was frowned upon. They usually received some education and training in accomplishments such as playing the piano but education was, first and foremost, a preparation for being a wife and mother. The pastimes of the middle-class lady were very separate from those of their menfolk who played very public roles. The female world was based in the more private atmosphere of the home. Margaret might well have found herself in such a position had she not married Henry Park in August 1872. He was an iron merchant and a partner in the old-established Wigan firm. Henry was also a Conservative who soon became involved in local politics. He rapidly gained a place on the council and his long period of office as Mayor in the 1880s gave Margaret, his second wife, an opportunity to put into practice much of the work she wanted to do. She was now permitted a public role (though of course an unpaid one) as a result of her husband's office and she was able to use effectively her considerable ability to organise. When Henry became Mayor, one councillor explained to a journal the value of a Mayor's wife who could help her husband's position:

It is said and I thoroughly agree with it, that before asking a gentleman to be Mayor you should ask what sort of a wife he has. We did not ask as to the suitability of the Mayoress, Mrs Park, but I make bold to say that she has proved herself most efficient.'

Municipal Review, February 1887

In fact, without wasting any time, Margaret threw herself wholeheartedly into her new job. She became involved in so many schemes that she later described herself as 'The Mother of Wigan'. She was able to use her position to advertise and raise subscriptions for schemes which interested her. One such project was the setting up of day nurseries. She arranged for the Countess of Lathom to address a meeting in the Council Chamber on this subject. Margaret hoped to set up these nurseries for the children of mill workers. She found that there was some opposition to the scheme and it ultimately failed. Doubtless she would have been saddened to know that a hundred years later the need to help working mothers is still

not really recognized. A new organisation to protect young girls, the White Cross Army also received Margaret's support as did a similar body, the Girls' Friendly Society (whose Liverpool branch President was the Countess of Lathom). It sought to bring together respectable young girls (and domestic servants in particular) and save them from temptation in the towns through moral and religious training. By 1885 it had 121 branches in England and Wales and Margaret helped to establish one branch in Wigan. She was President too of the local branch of the British Women's Temperance Association, another recent development and one which opposed the evils of drink. It tried to get women to set a good example to their husbands by not drinking alcohol. The Wigan branch included a number of pit women and miners' wives and this and her Sunday-school work enabled Margaret to get to know them. In a somewhat condescendng manner she referred to the pit lasses as 'noble women' who were 'doing their duty in the sphere of life in which God had placed them'.

Such organisations also provided a chance to build up a network of influential friends. One of these, Mrs Bright Lucas, was the President of the temperance organisation and she was also related to Walter McLaren, the Liberal MP for Crewe who helped organise the visit of the pit women to London with Margaret. He and other relatives of Mrs Lucas supported this visit, as did the Countess of Lathom. Yet another of Margaret's schemes was the Wigan Kyrle Society, formed to unite the well-to-do residents of Wigan to provide cheap concerts for the poor. Henry soon found that he had an effective partner in good works and achievements! He was a busy and active person, too. It was due to his efforts that Wigan got public baths and he had helped to organise Relief Funds during the cotton famine. However, one journal declared in 1887:

When all the Mayor's services are considered it is impossible to be surprised that he is, with one exception, the most popular inhabitant of Wigan.

That exception was, of course, Margaret Park. The *Sunday Chronicle* newspaper explained that she had a 'local reputation as leader of every movement for the benefit of the poor and suffering classes'. With what was possibly a deliberate pun, it added that she was seen as their 'trustworthy counsellor'.

The pit brow campaign

Given the interests of Margaret, it is not surprising that she defended the pit women's right to work. Having lived in the area for about 21 years and having known and visited pit lasses at work for about half of that time, she felt well qualified to intervene in 1886. She explained:

I have had much experience with miners and pit girls therefore. When I first came into this district I was shocked at the spectacle of the trousered women looking and working like men: but I soon recovered from the shock. I found the women healthy and honestly employed. I found them as a rule, equal in respectability to factory workers.'

Wigan Observer, 20 March 1886

Early in 1886 a new mines bill introduced by Gladstone's Liberal Government provided the opportunity for some people to argue that women should not be working at mines. Recently the hours that women were allowed to work in factories had been reduced, an example of the policy of what is called *protective legislation*; that is, laws passed with the purpose of protecting those who are not in a position to protect themselves. By the 1880s only about a quarter of all women worked in declared paid employment. Since women had limited legal rights it was felt that laws should be passed on their behalf. Yet, increasingly, a number of people, especially women, questioned the right to pass laws in this way. They felt that the women should have a say in deciding their own fate and that decisions should not be made for them, especially since they would not necessarily improve women's lives at all.

However, many saw it somewhat differently, arguing that the pit top was especially unsuitable for the female sex and believing that women should be protected from such work. Some critics even got confused and thought that women were still working underground. Some opposed the work though they knew little about it. Even those miners who publicly

attacked it (because they felt that women were taking men's rightful jobs) tended to come from areas which did not employ women pit brow workers. One Durham miner argued in Parliament that such work was fit only for strong muscular men and added that 'it was a woman's place to do much more delicate work than that'. There was one Lancashire member of the miners' union who spoke out against the work; however, this man, William Pickard, was no longer a working miner but an important mines official.

Indignant about the attack on pit women, local people in the Wigan area decided to join together and protest. The first meeting was held in a schoolroom in Pemberton, near Wigan in February 1886. It was called by the Rev. Harry Mitchell, the local Vicar whose charitable activities rivalled those of his friend Margaret Park. Numerous meetings were held over the next few months. At one, combined with a tea party (possibly the main attraction), 120 of the audience of 400 were pit women.

The Rev. Harry Mitchell (1847–1933) was the vicar of St Johns, Pemberton near Wigan for five years in the 1880s. At the end of 1886 he was chosen as the new vicar for nearby Prescot. He was continually active in parish causes.

31

Margaret chaired this meeting and she soon became the leader of the campaign. We first encountered her about to go to one of these meetings. She said that she feared the alternatives which faced pit women if they had to stop working. She even went so far as to say that the pit women were fit for no other occupation. Careful reading of her speeches shows the gulf that lay between her and women like Jane Brown.

At times Margaret made pit women's lives sound remarkably easy and trouble free. When asked about their clothes she replied that, 'a begrimed garment may cover a white heart, and I assert that the pit women are pure, industrious, well conducted'. She explained how their homes held great charms for them because they were out all day. She had watched them during the dinner hour and seen their rosy faces compared with those of the mill girls. Just as those against the work tended to generalise, claiming that all pit work was too heavy and unsuitable so that the women became wretched, immoral and unfeminine, so too was Margaret guilty of some generalisations and exaggeration. She summed up her view of the women as 'buxom, happy, modest and sensible looking'.

As the wife of a public figure well known in local and Conservative circles and with a business closely linked to the coal trade, Margaret knew a number of local coalowners and counted them amongst her friends. It was the wealthy colliery owner, the Earl of Crawford, who presented the Mayor and Mayoress with a jewelled silver plate for their services to the community. Not surprisingly, the coalowners wanted the women to remain in work – they were cheaper to employ than men and they were not members of the union. Margaret's prejudice against trades unions can be clearly seen in her speeches. She believed that they were inspired by jealousy and greed and she disliked their 'wonderful and mysterious powers for getting their own way, right or wrong'.

Organisation

Harry Mitchell compared the impact of the big meeting chaired by Margaret to that of

fired gunpowder. Realising the wider threat to women's work in general, he added that they were 'fighting a battle for the women of England generally'. The press soon echoed his views. In March *The Spectator* argued that the pit women's case was:

'the test case in which in all human probability the right of women to perform rough manual labour for wages and out of doors will for a long period be decided.'

Although the threat to the women's jobs did not become a reality in 1886 (no doubt due in part to Margaret's efforts, which included writing to the Home Secretary), the following year saw a renewed attack in Parliament and from the press. The Conservatives were now in power and they introduced another mines bill which once again provided an opportunity to attack the women. Twice the miners' union visited the new Home Secretary, Henry Matthews to protest against women pit workers. The following extract comes from a report of the miners' Conference of 1887, which discussed pit brow women.

The CHAIRMAN said that on former occasions they had passed resolutions against female labour, if not unanimously, yet by overwhelming majorities. At their interview with the Home Secretary, he, speaking, as he thought, the unanimous voice of the representatives of the miners of Great Britain, laid great stress on this point. Mr. Matthews put it pointedly to him, 'Are you unanimous?' and he replied, 'Yes; I think I have a right to say we are.' (Hear, hear.) To that statement there was no dissent, and he submitted that it was cutting the ground from under them, as miners' representatives, to have an attempt now made at the eleventh hour to rediscuss the matter, and to show that there was not general approval of the action they had taken. (Hear, hear.)

Mr. W. PICKARD said a part of Lancashire was placed in a very unpleasant position in regard to this matter. Parsons and ministers had got up a very strong agitation and had tried, but without avail, to get him on the platform in favour of female labour. Whatever might be the diversity of opinion in Lancashire, he thought they were honestly bound now to support their representatives in the action they had taken against female labour. (Hear, hear.)

Wigan Observer 27 April 1887

On 6 May a ban on all female miners was proposed in Parliament.

Margaret and her friends wasted no time. The MP Walter McLaren wrote to *The Times* seeking publicity for the women's cause and he suggested in Parliament that the women ought to visit the Home Secretary. He also wrote to Margaret and in response she called a meeting of colliery owners in the Council chamber. It is not clear exactly how the trip was organised. Margaret later claimed that the girls decided by ballot who was to go. It is probable though that the strong, healthy ones were singled out. The pit women were supposed to be paying for themselves (it cost £2 10s a head) and they repaid it over the weeks in small instalments from their pay. Evidence suggests that wealthy individuals also contributed towards the overall costs and Munby himself gave a pound. In order to see more closely what happened and understand the excitement of such a trip, let us follow Margaret and the pit lasses to London.

The trip to London

It is Monday 16 May 1887. Margaret arrives early at the Council chamber and with her husband, Harry Mitchell, Mr Dean (a colliery owner) and Mr Oakes (a local miners' agent who is sympathetic to women working) greets the pit lasses. Sixteen arrive, all 'tastefully attired' and accompanied by quite a crowd. They set off for the station taking with them trunks containing spare clothes and some pit costumes. Margaret is delighted to see how many local people have gathered to wish them luck as they board the 11.18 train for London. She is not used to travelling third-class and finds it somewhat uncomfortable, but she soon forgets this as she discoveres just how great a treat this journey is for the young women. The fact that it is a working day makes it even more fun!

At Warrington four more join the party, accompanied by Margaret's friend Mrs Burrows, the wife of the owner of an Atherton

The pit brow women's deputation in 1887

Name	Colliery or district	Age	Additional information
Sarah M'Gorian	Whitehaven	21	
Sarah Ray	Whitehaven	26	
Elizabeth Blaney	Whitehaven	29	
Annie Beswick	Bryn, nr Wigan	19	
Mary Jane Haseldon	Haydock, nr St Helens	16	Father had been ill for 2½ years and she had kept him, her mother and an orphan girl.
Mary Pennington	Ravenhead, St Helens	18	Tall, wore black. Been working for 5 years. Previously in service for short time but health suffered so went to pit glad to be back there.
Ann Lowe	Park Lane, Wigan	21?	Papers stated 21 but she was older. Married in 1887. Had worked many years on brow. Defended her work in a letter to *Wigan Observer*.
Mary Gore	Garswood Coal and Iron Co. Lancs	25	
Mary Smalley	Blundells, Pemberton	25	
Elizabeth Parker	Blundells, Pemberton	21	
Elizabeth Halliwell	Blundells, Pemberton	22/23	The tallest and finest according to Munby. He saw her again in September 1887 back in Wigan and gave her 1s.
Margaret Winstanley	Blundells, Pemberton	38	
Anne Smith	Aspull Moor, Wigan	23	A fine girl, according to Munby – sweet and gentle.
Jane Gibson	Aspull Moor, Wigan	21	
Ruth Hilton	Aspull Moor, Wigan	23	

colliery. The pit lasses are mainly young (the eldest is 38) and when they reach Euston station in London at 4.30 p.m. they join up with three more young women, the screen lasses who are representing the Whitehaven area in Cumberland.

Margaret has arranged for them to stay free at the Girls' Club and Home in Greek Street, Soho. The club's singing class greet them with songs and dancing. Margaret has rather more luxurious accommodation as the guest of the Lancashire colliery owner Colonel Blundell who has a town house in fashionable Mayfair. Blundells pit women have come on the trip and they have brought with them the special pit costume designed by his wife and provided free to employees. (See Polly Gee's photograph in the final chapter.)

At six o'clock the Lancashire visitors leave for an appointment at the Houses of Parliament. They are shown around and several MPs talk to them. Others who are generally interested in their cause have also gathered. One is the feminist Lydia Becker who is active in support of women's rights in Manchester.

Tuesday 17 May is, however, the day when the biggest crowd gathers. Margaret has explained to the pit women that whatever they do, they will be watched. And she is right. In the morning they march in procession through Regent Street, Oxford Street, along the Mall, across St James's Park and Whitehall to the Westminster Palace Hotel where they are due at 11 a.m. Already a number of newspaper reporters have gathered. One paper describes their appearance as 'a ladies' boarding school kind of procession'. The Blundells girls put on their blue costume, then it's off to the Home Office to put the case to Henry Matthews, the Home Secretary.

The women have a lot to say about the Wigan pits and they have already discussed how they feel about their jobs. Yet, when the time comes, they don't find that they have much opportunity to say anything. It seems as if their mere presence is what counts. There is a sort of correct order in which people seem to

The Home Office

be expected to talk and it's all very confusing. Walter McLaren makes a speech, then it's Margaret's turn. Here is part of her speech as reported in the local paper.

She had often visited the women on the brows for one purpose or another, and she found them intelligent, bright, open-faced, contented looking women and she had frequently said that for anyone in whom she was interested she would much prefer the work of the pit-brow to that of the mills or the fields. (Cheers.) They all looked plump and healthy; the outdoor work made them strong and vigorous, and many girls who had had to leave the mills through delicate health had become strong on the pit brow. It was well known that these women were very domesticated; their daily work being out of doors, they were glad when it was over to stay indoors and attend to home duties; while those poor girls who were all day amongst the heat and smells and din of machinery in mills were so glad to be out of doors at night that they ran a much greater risk of the immorality that was so wrongly attributed to the work at the pit-brow – work which was carried on in open daylight and in sight of everyone, and which normally terminated at five in the afternoon, or even earlier. In the present endeavour to maintain the right of these women to continue to obtain an honest livelihood in this way, they had the almost universal sympathy of the general public, and the cordial support of the press throughout the country. (Hear, hear.)

Wigan Observer, 20 May 1887

The *Liverpool Daily Post* comments:

'Never was a town better represented. It is no exaggeration to say that this Lady's admirable reading of the terse little speech she had prepared bore a very favourable comparison with even her Majesty's elocution, which is the highest compliment that can be paid to a lady in such a matter'.

She explains that 'as wife of the Mayor of the chief town in the coal trade of South-West Lancashire' she is in her right place as:

'leader in the movement for the preservation of their claim to earn an honest living in the way that suited them best in their circumstances and which had by this time become a tradition in their families'.

Other important people such as the Earl of Fortescue (President of the Society for the Employment of Women) also speak. The well-known supporter of women's rights, Josephine Butler talks briefly and a letter is read out, from a Welsh woman of 103 who had worked at the mines until she was 40. Four miners who (unlike the leaders of the miners' union), support the women, also speak in their favour.

In a way, the pit women are relieved that they don't have much chance to talk. Not only are they unused to public speaking but these people speak differently from themselves. Anyway, quite apart from accents, the London people seem to have difficulty understanding what the colliery folk are talking about! At one point one of the miners and the Home Secretary completely misunderstand each other and are talking at cross purposes. It's not until Margaret intervenes and explains that they are not disagreeing with each other but that one is referring to tubs and the other to wagons that they are able to continue. When the pit lass Elizabeth Halliwell interrupts to say how she disliked domestic service they all seem quite amused. Only she and one other girl say anything after coming all this way.

They do however feel that they must have made some sort of impression since the Home Secretary says he approves of them and their work. He comments on the Blundells costume,

'which I am bound to say looks rather Bulgarian than English; but it is perfectly modest, respectable and decent and for the work it seems to be a proper costume'.

The pit girls find this funny – what would he have said if he had seen their patched, faded cast-offs instead of the new, clean Blundells costume which only a few of them normally wear? And even a Blundells outfit could look mighty different after a day's coal dust!

Over a hundred of the leading figures in public causes have come along to watch the occasion. A further two hundred apologies have been sent from people sympathetic but unable to attend. On MP whose views are generally thought to be rather *radical* sums up:

'Pit mouth's work may not be very pleasant or very seemly for women, but I know nothing as unseemly or so unpleasant for women as an empty stomach and a family of starving children'.

Once the main event is over, the pit lasses are taken out to lunch. It has been very foggy earlier but it has now cleared and is a fine day. They leave the Home Office, once again marching in twos. Elizabeth Halliwell, the 22-year-old Blundells woman, dressed in her top coat, trousers and clogs is in the front. She is 5 feet 10 inches (1.78 m) tall and looks impressive, marching arm-in-arm with a very proud Munby. At last his two worlds have come together and he can publicly acknowledge his admiration for these women. He notices that the crowd stares, but is relieved that at least people do not laugh. Here is part of his account of the day.

Note. The 23 women whose names are overleaf were brought by train from Lancashire, on 16 May 1887, to London, by the Rev. Harry Mitchell Vicar of Prescot, and Mrs Park Mayoress of Wigan, and Mrs Burrows, wife of a coalowner. They came (at their own cost and that of their kin) as a deputation to the Home Secretary, to protest against the exclusion of women from pit work, which was proposed by the Trades Union *men*. The Hon. Maud Stanley housed them all at her Servants' Home in Greek Street Soho, and gave them tea. At 6 p.m., we marched them from Greek Street to the Houses of Parliament, Mrs Park and I leading. They were shown over both Houses, and introduced to many Members. All were comely, modest, robust; but the 3 finest girls were Ann Smith, Elizabeth Halliwell, and Ruth Hilton. At noon on the 17th, my old acquaintance the H.S. (Henry Matthews) received them all, with many ladies and M.P.s, at the Home Office. Afterwards, we walked down Whitehall, King Street, Broad Sanctuary, to 2 Westminster Chambers Victoria Street. Elizabeth Halliwell and I led the way, arm in arm: She in her pit breeches and clogshoon and sacking brat (apron) and topcoat and pitbonnet, her strong brown hands bare. 3 others so clad followed, and the rest in Sunday clothes. 'Yah' said Elizabeth to me, 'Ah'd coom 'ere agean abaht this job, sooneer till be tourn'd aht!'

The Illustrated London News's *view of the pit women's deputation from a photograph by Herbert Wragg of Wigan. An accompanying article added* 'The sympathy of sensible people not unmixed with amusement, wonder and a trifle of admiration has been recently expressed in favour of the sturdy Lancashire lasses'.

Munby's view of the day: a page from his diary.

Margaret is also relieved. She senses that they have won the day and that they have been a successful *pressure group*. She is feeling somewhat weary but she understands that, for the pit women, the most exciting part of their visit is just starting. After a welcome meal they set off on a tour of London. It is Jubilee year (50 years since Victoria became Queen) so there is plenty going on. They travel on the underground railway (a treat in itself) to the American Exhibition which has just opened at Earls Court to display America's inventions, arts and manufactured goods. It is much too crowded for Margaret's liking and she fears she may lose the women. They watch Buffalo Bill and walk through wigwams of Red Indians. One amusing new idea is a toboggan, which they try out. Then it's off to Baker Street. As is still the case today, a tour of London is not complete without seeing Madame Tussauds waxworks and, in particular, the Chamber of Horrors. Everywhere they receive special attentions – at the waxworks they are allowed to sit in Napoleon's carriage! A guided tour of St Pauls Cathedral follows. Margaret is trying to let them see as much as possible and decides that a riverboat trip is a good idea. They travel on the Thames as far as Charing Cross. Being quite a crowd, simply crossing the road is a major feat! However Margaret's influence is such that the police even hold up the traffic for them at Charing Cross. She then takes them to what she calls 'the very great treat' of seeing Mr and Mrs Blundell dressed for the Queen's drawing room. By this time however everybody is feeling rather tired. They also need to buy presents for those at home so they quickly call at a bazaar in Oxford Street before returning to the station. A special carriage has been laid on so that they don't have to change trains at Crewe.

Margaret feels exhausted but pleased. She admits that she had been a little worried before the trip. She believes that other people had expected to find the girls coarse, loud and vulgar and is relieved that they found them 'so gentle, sedate and nice'. As well as everyone behaving so well, she has achieved the main purpose of impressing the Home Secretary. Though Margaret still lacks the right to vote she has been determined to exert influence on Parliament in other ways. Henry Matthews has told her that the visit:

'would so influence public opinion that they would hear no more for many years of an attempt to interfere with an honest and praiseworthy industry either in Lancashire or anywhere else'.

The following extract from the Home Secretary's speech on the 1887 debate shows that he was as good as his word.

He had referred to the reports of Committees and had made the best inquiries he could from the inspectors who were in daily communication with these girls, and the conclusion he came to was that there was nothing to justify the House in interfering with an honest and healthy industry, which had been adopted by the deliberate preference of those engaged in it, to the universal satisfaction of their families and to the clergy who ministered to them.

Women's Suffrage Journal

The next month the clause in the mines bill was dropped and the women's work saved. Apart from banning them from moving heavy wagons, the 1887 Mines and Collieries Act allowed the pit women to continue doing all their old jobs and the new, easier ones that were developing as surface work became more mechanised. The colliery management and supporters of women's rights and in particular, Harry Mitchell, Margaret and the pit women were able to breathe a sigh of relief. And even though their role had been a limited one, at least this time, unlike 1842, colliery women had had rather more say in determining their own fate.

Margaret's later years

Soon after the events of 1887 the Parks moved to Southport. The strain of work had led to ill-health for Henry Park and he died in 1890.

Margaret too was ill at this time. Nevertheless, true to form, she soon resumed an active life. She helped run the Girls' Friendly Society in Southport, founded a Young Abstainers Union to encourage *temperance* among the town's youth and played an active part in church and charitable affairs. She and her son made a long trip to Australia to visit her sister in the winter of 1892 but the following year she was ill again and died on 17 December 1892, at the age of 58.

Commenting on her life, the *Southport Visitor* noted how systematic and extensive her private benevolence had been. She would be remembered for a long time, particularly by the working class, 'as a lady with a warm and generous heart'. This and another paper remarked on her work with the pit lasses, pointing out that she had gained for herself 'considerable prominence for the manner in which she had championed the cause of the pit brow women'.

5 Full circle

The story is not quite ended. Although the pit women and Margaret had been successful there was, some years later, a further attempt to stop women's pit brow work. This was in 1911 at a time of high unemployment, demands for a *minimum wage* for miners and when the *suffragettes* were getting considerable publicity. Once again Parliament considered banning women and once again there was a deputation. Forty-seven pit women from Lancashire (mainly from Wigan collieries) went to London after a huge meeting had been held for pit women at Wigan's skating rink. Drawing on the lessons of 1887, the Conservative Mayor Sam Wood (son of a coalowner), the Mayoress, a local vicar and a doctor accompanied the deputation. They too created a favourable impression and the Committee of the House of Commons which had declared itself opposed to female pit work, reversed its decision. When the new Mines Act was passed it still allowed all females over 13 to remain at the surface.

However, the demand for such work was gradually to decline. Apart from the growth of other, newer jobs for women (particularly in offices) and better communications which enabled people from colliery villages to travel further for work, the twentieth century was to see many surface jobs disappear as processes became more mechanised.

By the early twentieth century the work was less physically demanding than it had once been and about nine-tenths of the women were doing sorting work. There were temporary increases during war time: in 1918 for example there were over 11,300 pit women and many had joined the union, the National Federation of Women Workers. Numbers fell again in peace time and during this period some areas rather reluctantly admitted women to the miners' union. By the 1950s however, it was agreed that disabled miners should be given preference in surface jobs and elderly miners were also to be engaged rather than women. It was in the 1950s that most women left. In

some cases they were made redundant; more frequently they were simply not replaced when they retired. By 1953 under 1,000 remained – two thirds of them in Lancashire – and new methods of washing and sorting coal left fewer and fewer jobs. Added to this there were colliery closures generally. Coal was not seen then as a fuel with a future. The women's movement was not active and women did not resist redundancies. By the late 1960s there

Polly Gee in the Blundells costume she wore as a young girl on the 1911 deputation. Her recollections were recorded in the 1970s.

were no longer coalmining women in Lancashire, Scotland or Wales, though a few former pit women carried on as colliery cleaners and canteen workers. The very last two pit women left work at Whitehaven in Cumbria as recently as 1972. This was 130 years after the law had forbidden women to work underground. The *Sex Discrimination Act* reinforced the ban on women miners in late 1975.

However, in a small number of other countries women still work in mining. In India, poorly-paid women work at the surface. Chinese women led coal cutting teams in the 1970s but have recently stopped working below ground. In the United States, where there has not been a tradition of women miners (with the exception of isolated cases in tiny mines during the depression), women have recently entered mining. Strengthened by equal rights laws (though now threatened by the depressed state of the economy) they have worked in the

Barbara Angle: an American woman miner of the 1970s.

mines since the end of 1973. At present there are over three and a half thousand women miners, the successors to the British women of the early nineteenth century. They perform a whole range of jobs from face worker to being general labourers. They earn high wages though they work in conditions which are still dangerous. Nevertheless these conditions are a considerable improvement on those in which Jane Brown's mother and many other early Victorian coalmining women once worked.

A Chinese woman miner, Chiang Mei hsien, leader of a coal-cutting brigade in the 1970s.

40

Key dates

1833   **Factory Act** – forbids employment in textile mills (except lace) of children under 9; limits hours of those under 18; two hours daily education necessary
       Abolition of Slavery in British Colonies

1840   **Children's Employment Commission** established

1842   **Second Chartist petition**
       Mines and Collieries Act bans all children under 10 and females of any age from working underground in addition to other mining reforms
       Miners' Association – first national miners' union formed

1850   **First Mines Inspectors** appointed

1861–5   **American Civil War** Lancashire cotton famine

1865–7   **Select Committee on Mines**

1867   **Second Reform Act** adds 1 million male voters to the electorate; John Stuart Mill tries to get word 'man' in act changed to 'person'.

1870   **Education Act** (Elementary) creates school boards to provide new schools where necessary

1872   **Mines Act** forbids women's employment at night and after 2 p.m. on Saturdays; no girls under 10 to work on pit top

1873   **Agricultural Children's Act** bans those under 8 from working on farms

1878   **Factory and Workshops Act** consolidates earlier laws controlling hours and ages of females

1886   **Mines bill** introduced in Commons by Liberals; Lancashire people organise meetings in support of women's pit work

1887   **Conservative mines bill** poses further threat to pit women; meetings in many mining areas

       (May) Successful Deputation of 23 northern pit brow women and many supporters to Home Office
       (Sept) Mines and Collieries Act passed: allows women's pit work to continue, age of entry raised to 12, women not to move heavy wagons

1888   **Match Girls' strike**

1911   **Women's Suffrage demonstrations**
       New Mines bill – further threat to pit women
       Second pit women's Deputation – double original size, also successful

1914–18   **First World War** – temporary dramatic increase in numbers of pit women

1918   **Limited Vote** for women over 30

1920s   **New coal washing methods** reduce demand for pit women

1928   **Women over 21 get the vote**

1939–45   **Second World War**

1954   **Mines and Quarries Act** reconfirms ban on women working underground

1950s to early 1960s
       Majority of pit brow women leave
       NUM and NCB agree priority should be given to elderly and disabled miners for remaining surface work

1972   **Last two British pit women** leave work in Whitehaven

1973   **(Dec.) First two modern American women miners** start work below ground in Kentucky

1975   **Sex Discrimination Act** introduced to provide equal opportunities for women, but makes a significant exception in the case of coalmining and does not recommend repeal of the ban on British women working *in* mines.

Glossary

barrister a trained lawyer who works in the higher courts of law

bearer a woman who bore coal on her back in Scotland

belt and chain harness worn by women and children underground

cannel (as in 'Ince Hall Coal and Cannel Company') a type of coal found in Wigan (and other areas) which burns brightly; used in gas making

carter/trammer boys, girls and women pulled tubs of coal, but generally lads were used as carters in charge of horse-drawn carts/trams

Chartism the first national working-class movement (1836–58), through its 6-point Charter sought the vote and other political rights for all adult men, ceased to be mass movement after 1848

damp firedamp (methane gas) causes explosions

deputation people arguing publicly for a cause through a group stating their case

drawer/putter woman or child who drew or pulled tubs of coal underground

drift a mine that can be entered via a slope instead of a shaft

Ecclesiastic Commission a permanent body set up in 1836 to administer and improve the affairs of the Church of England

elementary education provision of basic education for children – see 1870 Act in Key dates

face the place where the coal is cut out

hewer (sometimes called a getter) the miner who cuts out the coal – done by hand in the nineteenth century

Methodist a supporter of the religious organisation started by John Wesley in the eighteenth century

minimum wage the principle that all should earn at least an agreed basic wage

Nonconformist Methodists and other Protestants who follow their own beliefs rather than those of the Church of England and worship in their own chapels

picking belts travelling bands at foot of screens where men, lads or women handpick coal

pressure group a body which exists to publicise or campaign for a particular cause

protective legislation based on the belief that certain people who are not in a position to help themselves should have laws passed for their own good; here it refers to restricting or banning women's employment in certain industries

radical a person wanting basic changes in society or an adjective from this

riddle a sieve for sorting coal by hand

Royal Commission an enquiry into a subject authorised by the monarch

screens the surface onto which coal was tipped for sorting

shaft a vertical tunnel linking the surface or ground level with underground

slackwasher person who works in place where small coal is washed clean

sub-contractor person employing others who is already working for someone else

Suffragettes women who wanted the vote and drew the public's attention to their cause – sometimes by breaking the law

surface colliery area *above* ground where people do mining work

temperance the habit of not drinking alcohol on principle

tippler the machine into which a full tub of coal would be placed and then tipped out on to the screen

trapper child who opened and closed ventilation doors underground

windlass a wooden roller with a handle which raised and lowered baskets of coal and sometimes people

women's movement the supporters of equal rights for women in society; in the nineteenth century efforts were largely directed towards obtaining the vote for women

Suggestions for study

1 What other sources can you think of which might be helpful in finding out about women miners? (If you live in a mining area find out whether women ever worked at the local pits.)

2 Why do you think the ban on women underground miners was delayed until 1842 when women had been working for centuries?

3 What uses did coal have in the nineteenth century?

4 Imagine a day in the life of a woman who worked down a mine and describe it.

5 Why did women work illegally after 1842?

6 What kind of jobs were there on the surface in the second-half of the nineteenth century?

7 Describe or draw the inside of a miner's cottage.

8 What jobs would a pit lass have had to do at home?

9 How different do you think surface work was from work below ground?

10 Describe an imaginary conversation between Jane Brown and her mother where her mother tells her about her early life as a girl miner.

11 How do you think Mrs Brown spent Jane's wages?

12 Imagine a conversation between Jane and Munby in Wigan market. What might they have said?

13 Why did some people object to pit women wearing trousers?

14 Compare the working day of a mill girl and a pit girl. Which work might you have preferred?

15 Why did many pit girls not study or go to church on Sundays?

16 What do you think the manager of the Ince Hall colliery might have said to the Mining Committee when he was asked if the work was suitable for women?

17 Write a speech for Margaret Park to deliver at a meeting in support of women's pit work.

18 Why did the miners' union oppose the women's work?

19 Would you have supported the pit women? Give your reasons.

20 Write a newspaper report of the deputation to the Home Office.

21 Imagine you are one of the pit girls on the deputation. Write an account of the visit to London
or Imagine you are a young lad who has just started pit work. What do you think of women working at your pit?

22 Do you think attitudes towards women's work have changed much since the nineteenth century?

23 Do you think women should be allowed to work in British coalmines today?

Further reading

Introductory

General

C. Adams, *Ordinary Lives*, Virago 1982

R. M. Evans, *Children Working Underground*, National Museum of Wales 1979

P. Rooke, *Women's Rights*, Wayland Documentary History 1972

E. Royston Pike, *Human Documents of the Industrial Revolution*, Allen and Unwin 1970 ed

A. M. Turnbull, *Women With a Past*, Women's Research and Resources Centre 1980

Folk song

R. Palmer (ed.), *Poverty Knock*, Cambridge University Press 1974

Photographs

A. Burton, *The Miners*, Futura 1976

M. Hiley, *Victorian Working Women*, Gordon Fraser 1979

Specific Areas

Wales:

M. Davies, *Pembrokeshire Children in History*, Gomer 1983

R. M. Evans, *Children in the Mines 1840–2*, National Museum of Wales 1972

R. Keen, *Coalface*, National Museum of Wales 1982 ed

Lancashire:

J. Lane, D. Anderson, *Mines and Miners of south Lancashire*, Pub. D. Anderson 1981

Wigan Record Office, *Those Dark Satanic Mills*, 1981

Black Country:

S. Price *Twopence a Tub*, (a novel), Faber and Faber 1975

Shropshire:

Ironbridge Gorge Museum, *Shropshire Pit Girls*

More advanced

Arts Council, *British Mining in Art* 1983

G. Battiscombe, *Shaftesbury*, Constable 1974

D. Beddoe, *Discovering Women's History*, Pandora 1983

J. Benson, *British Coalminers in the Nineteenth Century*, Gill and Macmillan 1980

M. Cruikshank, *Children and Industry*, Manchester University Press 1981

D. Gorham, *The Victorian Girl and the Feminine Ideal*, Croom Helm 1982

A. R. Griffin, *The Collier*, Shire Publications 1982

History Workshop Journal no. 8 Autumn 1979: article by S. Alexander, A. Davin, E. Hostettler 'Labouring Women'

History Today, 'What is Women's History?' vol 35, June 1985

E. Hopkins, *A Social History of the English Working Classes*, Edward Arnold 1979

D. Hudson, *Munby, Man of Two Worlds*, John Murray, 1972

A. V. John, *By the Sweat of their Brow. Women Workers at Victorian Coal Mines*. Croom Helm 1980 and Routledge 1984

B. Lewis, *Coal Mining in the Eighteenth and Nineteenth Centuries*, Longman 1971

J. Liddington, J. Norris, *One Hand Tied Behind Us*, Virago 1978

N. Longmate, *The Hungry Mills*, Temple Smith 1978

S. Rowbotham, *Hidden From History*, Pluto 1973 ed

'The collier lass'

My name's Pol - ly Par - ker, I come o'er from Wor - sley. My fa - ther and
moth - er work in the coal mine. ___ Our fam - il - y's large, we have got sev - en
chil - dren. So I am ob - liged to work in the same mine. As
this is my for - tune, I know you'll feel sor - ry That in such em - ploy-ment my
days I shall pass. I keep up my spir - its, I sing and look
mer - ry, Al - though I am but a poor col - lier lass.

2 By the greatest of dangers each day I'm surrounded;
I hang in the air by a rope or a chain.
The mine may fall in, I may be killed or wounded,
May perish by damp or the fire of the train.
And what would you do if it weren't for our labour?
In wretched starvation your days you would pass,
While we could provide you with life's greatest blessing –
Then do not despise the poor collier lass.

3 Now all the day long you may say we are buried,
Deprived of the light and the warmth of the sun;
And often at nights from our bed we are hurried:
The water is in and then barefoot we run.
And though we go ragged and black are our faces,
As kind and as free as the best we'll be found;
Our hearts are as white as your lords, in fine places,
Although we're poor colliers that work underground.

4 I'm growing up fast, now, one way or another;
There's a collier lad strangely runs in my mind.
In spite of the talking of father and mother,
I think I should marry if he was inclined.
But should he prove surly and would not befriend me,
Another and better chance may come to pass.
My friends here, I know, to him will commend me,
And I'll be no longer a collier lass.

44